CW00589764

ISBN: 978 1717863 898

A. Hawkins

(SENCO/DSL who hates hunting for the document she needs and would prefer a printed book!)

Working Together to Safeguard Children

A guide to inter-agency working to safeguard and promote the welfare of children

July 2018

Contents

Introduction

Nothing is more important than children's welfare. Children[1] who need help and protection deserve high quality and effective support as soon as a need is identified.

We want a system that responds to the needs and interests of children and families and not the other way around. In such a system, practitioners[2] will be clear about what is required of them individually, and how they need to work together in partnership with others.

Whilst it is parents and carers who have primary care for their children, local authorities, working with partner organisations and agencies, have specific duties to safeguard and promote the welfare of all children in their area. The Children Acts of 1989 and 2004 set out specific duties: section 17 of the Children Act 1989 puts a duty on the local authority to provide services to children in need in their area, regardless of where they are found; section 47 of the same Act requires local authorities to undertake enquiries if they believe a child has suffered or is likely to suffer significant harm. The Director of Children's Services and Lead Member for Children's Services in local authorities are the key points of professional and political accountability, with responsibility for the effective delivery of these functions.

These duties placed on the local authority can only be discharged with the full co-operation of other partners, many of whom have individual duties when carrying out their functions under section 11 of the Children Act 2004 (see chapter 2). Under section 10 of the same Act, the local authority is under a duty to make arrangements to promote co-operation between itself and organisations and agencies to improve the wellbeing of local children (see chapter 1). This co-operation should exist and be effective at all levels of an organisation, from strategic level through to operational delivery.

The Children Act 2004, as amended by the Children and Social Work Act 2017, strengthens this already important relationship by placing new duties on key agencies in a local area. Specifically the police, clinical commissioning groups and the local authority are under a duty to make arrangements to work together, and with other partners locally, to safeguard and promote the welfare of all children in their area.

Everyone who comes into contact with children and families has a role to play.

Safeguarding and promoting the welfare of children is defined for the purposes of this guidance as:

---

[1] In this document, a child is defined as anyone who has not yet reached their 18th birthday. 'Children' therefore means 'children and young people' throughout.
[2] The term 'practitioners' is used throughout the guidance to refer to individuals who work with children and their families in any capacity.

- protecting children from maltreatment

- preventing impairment of children's health or development

- ensuring that children grow up in circumstances consistent with the provision of safe and effective care

- taking action to enable all children to have the best outcomes

About this guidance

1.   This guidance covers:

- the legislative requirements placed on individual services

- a framework for the three local safeguarding partners (the local authority; a clinical commissioning group for an area, any part of which falls within the local authority; and the chief officer of police for a police area, any part of which falls within the local authority area) to make arrangements to work together to safeguard and promote the welfare of local children including identifying and responding to their needs

- the framework for the two child death review partners (the local authority and any clinical commissioning group for an area, any part of which falls within the local authority) to make arrangements to review all deaths of children normally resident in the local area, and if they consider it appropriate, for those not normally resident in the area

2.   This document replaces Working Together to Safeguard Children (2015). Links to relevant supplementary guidance that practitioners should consider alongside this guidance can be found at Appendix B.

What is the status of this guidance?

3.   This guidance applies to all organisations and agencies who have functions relating to children. Specifically, this guidance applies to all local authorities, clinical commissioning groups, police and all other organisations and agencies as set out in chapter 2.

4.   It applies, in its entirety, to all schools.

5.   It applies to all children up to the age of 18 years whether living with their families, in state care, or living independently.

6.   This document should be complied with unless exceptional circumstances arise.

7. The guidance is issued under:

- section 7 of the Local Authority Social Services Act 1970, which requires local authorities in their social services functions to act under the general guidance of the Secretary of State

- section 10(8) of the Children Act 2004, which requires each person or organisation to which the section 10 duty applies to have regard to any guidance given to them by the Secretary of State

- section 11(4) of the Children Act 2004 which requires each person or organisation to which the section 11 duty applies to have regard to any guidance given to them by the Secretary of State

- section 16B(7) of the Children Act 2004, as amended by the Children and Social Work Act 2017, which states that the Child Safeguarding Practice Review Panel must have regard to any guidance given by the Secretary of State in connection with its functions

- section 16C(2) of the Children Act 2004, as amended by the Children and Social Work Act 2017, which states that local authorities must have regard to any guidance given by the Secretary of State in connection with their functions relating to notifications

- section 16K of the Children Act 2004, as amended by the Children and Social Work Act 2017, which states that the safeguarding partners and relevant agencies for a local authority area in England must have regard to any guidance given by the Secretary of State in connection with their functions under sections 16E-16J of the Act

- section 16Q of the Children Act 2004, as amended by the Children and Social Work Act 2017, which states that the child death review partners for a local authority area in England must have regard to any guidance given by the Secretary of State in connection with their functions under sections 16M-16P of the Act

- section 175(4) of the Education Act 2002, which states that governing bodies of maintained schools (including maintained nursery schools), further education institutions and management committees of pupil referral units must have regard to any guidance given by the Secretary of State

- paragraph 7(b) of the Schedule to the Education (Independent School Standards) Regulations 2014, made under sections 94(1) and (2) of the Education and Skills Act 2008, which states that the arrangements to safeguard or promote the welfare of pupils made by the proprietors of independent schools (including academies or free schools) or alternative provision academies must have regard to any guidance given by the Secretary of State

- paragraph 3 of the Schedule to the Non-Maintained Special Schools (England) Regulations 2015, made under section 342 of the Education Act 1996, which requires arrangements for safeguarding and promoting the health, safety and welfare of pupils in non-maintained special schools to have regard to any guidance published on such issues

Who is this guidance for?

8.   This statutory guidance should be read and followed by strategic and senior leaders and frontline practitioners of all organisations and agencies as set out in chapter 2 of this document. At a strategic level, this includes local authority Chief Executives, Directors of Children's Services, chief officers of police and clinical commissioning groups and other senior leaders within organisations and agencies that commission and provide services for children and families. Members of the Child Safeguarding Practice Review Panel (see chapter 4) should also read and follow this guidance.

9.   This guidance focuses on the core legal requirements, making it clear what individuals, organisations and agencies must and should do to keep children safe. In doing so, it seeks to emphasise that effective safeguarding is achieved by putting children at the centre of the system and by every individual and agency playing their full part.

A child-centred approach to safeguarding

10.   This child centred approach is fundamental to safeguarding and promoting the welfare of every child. A child centred approach means keeping the child in focus when making decisions about their lives and working in partnership with them and their families.

11.   All practitioners should follow the principles of the Children Acts 1989 and 2004 - that state that the welfare of children is paramount and that they are best looked after within their families, with their parents playing a full part in their lives, unless compulsory intervention in family life is necessary.

12.   Children may be vulnerable to neglect and abuse or exploitation from within their family and from individuals they come across in their day-to-day lives. These threats can take a variety of different forms, including: sexual, physical and emotional abuse; neglect; exploitation by criminal gangs and organised crime groups; trafficking; online abuse; sexual exploitation and the influences of extremism leading to radicalisation. Whatever the form of abuse or neglect, practitioners should put the needs of children first when determining what action to take.

13. Children are clear about what they want from an effective safeguarding system. <u>These asks from children should guide the behaviour of practitioners.</u>

Children have said that they need

- vigilance: to have adults notice when things are troubling them

- understanding and action: to understand what is happening; to be heard and understood; and to have that understanding acted upon

- stability: to be able to develop an ongoing stable relationship of trust with those helping them

- respect: to be treated with the expectation that they are competent rather than not

- information and engagement: to be informed about and involved in procedures, decisions, concerns and plans

- explanation: to be informed of the outcome of assessments and decisions and reasons when their views have not met with a positive response

- support: to be provided with support in their own right as well as a member of their family

- advocacy: to be provided with advocacy to assist them in putting forward their views

- protection: to be protected against all forms of abuse and discrimination and the right to special protection and help if a refugee

14. Anyone working with children should see and speak to the child; listen to what they say; take their views seriously; and work with them and their families collaboratively when deciding how to support their needs. Special provision should be put in place to support dialogue with children who have communication difficulties, unaccompanied children, refugees and those children who are victims of modern slavery and/or trafficking. This child-centred approach is supported by:

- the Children Act 1989. This Act requires local authorities to give due regard to a child's wishes when determining what services to provide under section 17 and before making decisions about action to be taken to protect individual children under section 47. These duties complement requirements relating to the wishes and feelings of children who are, or may be, looked-after (section 22(4)), including those who are provided with accommodation under section 20 and children taken into police protection (section 46(3)(d))

- the Equality Act 2010, which puts a responsibility on public authorities to have due regard to the need to eliminate discrimination and promote equality of opportunity. This applies to the process of identification of need and risk faced by the individual child and the process of assessment. No child or group of children must be treated any less favourably than others in being able to access effective services which meet their particular needs

- the United Nations Convention on the Rights of the Child (UNCRC)[3]. This is an international agreement that protects the rights of children and provides a child-centred framework for the development of services to children. The UK Government ratified the UNCRC in 1991 and, by doing so, recognises children's rights to expression and receiving information

15.   In addition to practitioners shaping support around the needs of individual children, local organisations and agencies should have a clear understanding of the collective needs of children locally when commissioning effective services. As part of that process, the Director of Public Health should ensure that the needs of children are a key part of the Joint Strategic Needs Assessment (JSNA) developed by the Health and wellbeing board. Safeguarding partners should use this assessment to help them understand the prevalence and contexts of need, including specific needs relating to disabled children and those relating to abuse and neglect, which in turn should help shape services.

A co-ordinated approach – safeguarding is everyone's responsibility

16.   Everyone who works with children has a responsibility for keeping them safe. No single practitioner can have a full picture of a child's needs and circumstances and, if children and families are to receive the right help at the right time, everyone who comes into contact with them has a role to play in identifying concerns, sharing information and taking prompt action.

17.   In order that organisations, agencies and practitioners collaborate effectively, it is vital that everyone working with children and families, including those who work with parents/carers, understands the role they should play and the role of other practitioners. They should be aware of, and comply with, the published arrangements set out by the local safeguarding partners.

18.   This statutory guidance sets out key roles for individual organisations and agencies to deliver effective arrangements for safeguarding. It is essential that these arrangements are strongly led and promoted at a local level, specifically by local area leaders, including local authority Chief Executives and Lead Members of Children's Services, Mayors, the

---

[3] United Nations Convention on the Rights of the Child

Police and Crime Commissioner and through the commitment of chief officers in all organisations and agencies, in particular those representing the three safeguarding partners. These are Directors of Children's Services, Chief Constables of police and Accountable Officers and/or Chief Nurses of clinical commissioning groups.

19.   The local authority and its social workers have specific roles and responsibilities to lead the statutory assessment of children in need (section 17, Children Act 1989) and to lead child protection enquiries (section 47, Children Act 1989). It is crucial that social workers are supported through effective supervision arrangements by practice leaders[4] and practice supervisors, as defined under the National Assessment and Accreditation system, who have the lead role in overseeing the quality of social work practice. Designated Principal Social Workers have a key role in developing the practice and the practice methodology that underpins direct work with children and families.

---

[4] Practice leaders as defined by the relevant knowledge and skills statement issued by the DfE have a key role to ensure that decisions about children are made according to this guidance.

Chapter 1: Assessing need and providing help

Early help

1.   Providing early help is more effective in promoting the welfare of children than reacting later. Early help means providing support as soon as a problem emerges, at any point in a child's life, from the foundation years through to the teenage years. Early help can also prevent further problems arising; for example, if it is provided as part of a support plan where a child has returned home to their family from care, or in families where there are emerging parental mental health issues or drug and alcohol misuse.

2.   Effective early help relies upon local organisations and agencies working together to:

☐   identify children and families who would benefit from early help

☐   undertake an assessment of the need for early help

☐   provide targeted early help services to address the assessed needs of a child and their family which focuses on activity to improve the outcomes for the child

3.   Local authorities, under section 10 of the Children Act 2004[5], have a responsibility to promote inter-agency co-operation to improve the welfare of all children.

Identifying children and families who would benefit from early help

4.   Local organisations and agencies should have in place effective ways to identify emerging problems and potential unmet needs of individual children and families. Local authorities should work with organisations and agencies to develop joined-up early help services based on a clear understanding of local needs. This requires all practitioners, including those in universal services and those providing services to adults with children, to understand their role in identifying emerging problems and to share information with other practitioners to support early identification and assessment.

5.   Multi-agency training will be important in supporting this collective understanding of local need. Practitioners working in both universal services and specialist services have a responsibility to identify the symptoms and triggers of abuse and neglect, to share that information and provide children with the help they need. To be effective, practitioners need to continue to develop their knowledge and skills in this area and be aware of the

---

[5] Section 10 of the Children Act 2004 requires each local authority to make arrangements to promote co-operation between the authority, each of the authority's relevant partners and such other persons or bodies working with children in the local authority's area as the authority considers appropriate.

new and emerging threats, including online abuse, grooming, sexual exploitation and radicalisation. To enable this, the three safeguarding partners should consider what training is needed locally and how they will monitor and evaluate the effectiveness of any training they commission.

6.   Practitioners should, in particular, be alert to the potential need for early help for a child who:

- is disabled and has specific additional needs[6]

- has special educational needs (whether or not they have a statutory Education, Health and Care Plan)

- is a young carer

- is showing signs of being drawn into anti-social or criminal behaviour, including gang involvement and association with organised crime groups

- is frequently missing/goes missing from care or from home[7]

- is at risk of modern slavery, trafficking or exploitation

- is at risk of being radicalised or exploited

- is in a family circumstance presenting challenges for the child, such as drug and alcohol misuse, adult mental health issues and domestic abuse

- is misusing drugs or alcohol themselves

- has returned home to their family from care[8]

- is a privately fostered child[9]

Effective assessment of the need for early help.

7.   Children and families may need support from a wide range of local organisations and agencies. Where a child and family would benefit from co-ordinated support from more than one organisation or agency (e.g. education, health, housing, police) there should be an inter-agency assessment. These early help assessments should be evidence-based, be clear about the action to be taken and services to be provided and

---

[6] Part 3 of the Children and Families Act 2014 promotes the physical, mental health and emotional wellbeing of children and young people with special educational needs or disabilities
[7] Children who run away or go missing from care (2014)
[8] Children return home to their families from local authority care under a range of circumstances. These circumstances and the related local authority duties are set out in flow chart 6
[9] Private fostering occurs when a child under the age of 16 (under 18, if disabled) is provided with care and accommodation by a person who is not a parent, person with parental responsibility for them or a relative in their own home. A child is not privately fostered if the person caring for and accommodating them has done so for less than 28 days and does not intend to do so for longer.

identify what help the child and family require to prevent needs escalating to a point where intervention would be needed through a statutory assessment under the Children Act 1989.

8.   A lead practitioner should undertake the assessment, provide help to the child and family, act as an advocate on their behalf and co-ordinate the delivery of support services. A GP, family support worker, school nurse, teacher, health visitor and/or special educational needs co-ordinator could undertake the lead practitioner role. Decisions about who should be the lead practitioner should be taken on a case-by-case basis and should be informed by the child and their family.

9.   For an early help assessment to be effective:

- it should be undertaken with the agreement of the child and their parents or carers, involving the child and family as well as all the practitioners who are working with them. It should take account of the child's wishes and feelings wherever possible, their age, family circumstances and the wider community context in which they are living

- practitioners should be able to discuss concerns they may have about a child and family with a social worker in the local authority. Local authority children's social care should set out the process for how this will happen

10.   In cases where consent is not given for an early help assessment, practitioners should consider how the needs of the child might be met. If at any time it is considered that the child may be a child in need, as defined in the Children Act 1989, or that the child has suffered significant harm or is likely to do so, a referral should be made immediately to local authority children's social care. This referral can be made by any practitioner.

Provision of effective early help services

11.   The provision of early help services should form part of a continuum of support to respond to the different levels of need of individual children and families.

12.   Local areas should have a comprehensive range of effective, evidence-based services in place to address assessed needs early. The early help on offer should draw upon any local assessment of need, including the JSNA and the latest evidence of the effectiveness of early help programmes. In addition to high quality support in universal services, specific local early help services will typically include family and parenting programmes, assistance with health issues, including mental health, responses to emerging thematic concerns in extra-familial contexts, and help for emerging problems relating to domestic abuse, drug or alcohol misuse by an adult or a child. Services may also focus on improving family functioning and building the family's own capability to solve

problems. This should be done within a structured, evidence-based framework involving regular review to ensure that real progress is being made. Some of these services may be delivered to parents but should always be evaluated to demonstrate the impact they are having on the outcomes for the child.

Accessing help and services

13.   Where a child's need is relatively low level, individual services and universal services may be able to take swift action. Where there are more complex needs, help may be provided under section 17 of the Children Act 1989 (children in need). Where there are child protection concerns (reasonable cause to suspect a child is suffering or likely to suffer significant harm) local authority social care services must make enquiries and decide if any action must be taken under section 47 of the Children Act 1989.

14.   It is important that there are clear criteria amongst all organisations and agencies working with children and families for taking action and providing help across this full continuum to ensure that services are commissioned effectively and that the right help is given to the child at the right time[10].

15.   In making their local arrangements, the safeguarding partners should agree with their relevant agencies the levels for the different types of assessment and services to be commissioned and delivered. This should include services for children who have suffered or are likely to suffer abuse and neglect whether from within the family or from external threats. This should also include services for disabled children and be aligned with the short breaks services statement[11].

16.   The safeguarding partners should publish a threshold document, which sets out the local criteria for action in a way that is transparent, accessible and easily understood. This should include:

☐ the process for the early help assessment and the type and level of early help services to be provided

- the criteria, including the level of need, for when a case should be referred to local authority children's social care for assessment and for statutory services under:

  - section 17 of the Children Act 1989 (children in need)

  - section 47 of the Children Act 1989 (reasonable cause to suspect a child is suffering or likely to suffer significant harm)

---

[10] Guidance on specific safeguarding concerns can be found in Appendix B.
[11] Required under the Breaks for Carers of Disabled Children Regulations 2011.

- section 31 of the Children Act 1989 (care and supervision orders)

- section 20 of the Children Act 1989 (duty to accommodate a child)

☐ clear procedures and processes for cases relating to:

- the abuse, neglect and exploitation of children

- children managed within the youth secure estate

- disabled children

Referral

17. Anyone who has concerns about a child's welfare should make a referral to local authority children's social care and should do so immediately if there is a concern that the child is suffering significant harm or is likely to do so. Practitioners who make a referral should always follow up their concerns if they are not satisfied with the response.

18. Local authority children's social care has the responsibility for clarifying the process for referrals. This includes specific arrangements for referrals in areas where there are secure youth establishments.

19. Within local authorities, children's social care should act as the principal point of contact for safeguarding concerns relating to children. As well as protocols for practitioners working with children and families, contact details should be signposted clearly so that children, parents and other family members are aware of who they can contact if they wish to make a referral, require advice and/or support.

20. When practitioners refer a child, they should include any information they have on the child's developmental needs, the capacity of the child's parents or carers to meet those needs and any external factors that may be undermining their capacity to parent. This information may be included in any assessment, including an early help assessment, which may have been carried out prior to a referral into local authority children's social care. Where an early help assessment has already been undertaken, it should be used to support a referral to local authority children's social care; however, this is not a prerequisite for making a referral.

21. If practitioners have concerns that a child may be a potential victim of modern slavery or human trafficking then a referral should be made to the National Referral Mechanism[12], as soon as possible.

---

[12] National Referral Mechanism.

22.   Feedback should be given by local authority children's social care to the referrer on the decisions taken. Where appropriate, this feedback should include the reasons why a case may not meet the statutory threshold and offer suggestions for other sources of more suitable support. Practitioners should always follow up their concerns if they are not satisfied with the local authority children's social care response and should escalate their concerns if they remain dissatisfied.

Information sharing

23.   Effective sharing of information between practitioners and local organisations and agencies is essential for early identification of need, assessment and service provision to keep children safe. Serious case reviews (SCRs[13]) have highlighted that missed opportunities to record, understand the significance of and share information in a timely manner can have severe consequences for the safety and welfare of children.

24.   Practitioners should be proactive in sharing information as early as possible to help identify, assess and respond to risks or concerns about the safety and welfare of children, whether this is when problems are first emerging, or where a child is already known to local authority children's social care (e.g. they are being supported as a child in need or have a child protection plan). Practitioners should be alert to sharing important information about any adults with whom that child has contact, which may impact the child's safety or welfare.

25.   Information sharing is also essential for the identification of patterns of behaviour when a child has gone missing, when multiple children appear associated to the same context or locations of risk, or in relation to children in the secure estate where there may be multiple local authorities involved in a child's care. It will be for local safeguarding partners to consider how they will build positive relationships with other local areas to ensure that relevant information is shared in a timely and proportionate way.

26.   Fears about sharing information <u>must not be allowed</u> to stand in the way of the need to promote the welfare, and protect the safety, of children, which must always be the paramount concern. To ensure effective safeguarding arrangements:

- all organisations and agencies should have arrangements in place that set out clearly the processes and the principles for sharing information. The arrangement should cover how information will be shared within their own organisation/agency; and with others who may be involved in a child's life

---

[13] Pathways to harm, pathways to protection: a triennial analysis of serious case reviews, 2011 to 2014

- all practitioners should not assume that someone else will pass on information that they think may be critical to keeping a child safe. If a practitioner has concerns about a child's welfare and considers that they may be a child in need or that the child has suffered or is likely to suffer significant harm, then they should share the information with local authority children's social care and/or the police. All practitioners should be particularly alert to the importance of sharing information when a child moves from one local authority into another, due to the risk that knowledge pertinent to keeping a child safe could be lost

- all practitioners should aim to gain consent to share information, but should be mindful of situations where to do so would place a child at increased risk of harm. Information may be shared without consent if a practitioner has reason to believe that there is good reason to do so, and that the sharing of information will enhance the safeguarding of a child in a timely manner. When decisions are made to share or withhold information, practitioners should record who has been given the information and why

27.   Practitioners must have due regard to the relevant data protection principles which allow them to share personal information, as provided for in the Data Protection Act 2018 and the General Data Protection Regulation (GDPR). To share information effectively:

- all practitioners should be confident of the processing conditions under the Data Protection Act 2018 and the GDPR which allow them to store and share information for safeguarding purposes, including information which is sensitive and personal, and should be treated as 'special category personal data'

- where practitioners need to share special category personal data, they should be aware that the Data Protection Act 2018 contains 'safeguarding of children and individuals at risk' as a processing condition that allows practitioners to share information. This includes allowing practitioners to share information without consent, if it is not possible to gain consent, it cannot be reasonably expected that a practitioner gains consent, or if to gain consent would place a child at risk

Myth-busting guide to information sharing

Sharing information enables practitioners and agencies to identify and provide appropriate services that safeguard and promote the welfare of children. Below are common myths that may hinder effective information sharing.

Data protection legislation is a barrier to sharing information

No – the Data Protection Act 2018 and GDPR do not prohibit the collection and sharing of personal information, but rather provide a framework to ensure that personal information is shared appropriately. In particular, the Data Protection Act 2018 balances the rights of the information subject (the individual whom the information is about) and the possible need to share information about them.

Consent is always needed to share personal information

No – you do not necessarily need consent to share personal information. Wherever possible, you should seek consent and be open and honest with the individual from the outset as to why, what, how and with whom, their information will be shared. You should seek consent where an individual may not expect their information to be passed on. When you gain consent to share information, it must be explicit, and freely given. There may be some circumstances where it is not appropriate to seek consent, because the individual cannot give consent, or it is not reasonable to obtain consent, or because to gain consent would put a child's or young person's safety at risk.

Personal information collected by one organisation/agency cannot be disclosed to another

No – this is not the case, unless the information is to be used for a purpose incompatible with the purpose for which it was originally collected. In the case of children in need, or children at risk of significant harm, it is difficult to foresee circumstances where information law would be a barrier to sharing personal information with other practitioners[14].

The common law duty of confidence and the Human Rights Act 1998 prevent the sharing of personal information

No – this is not the case. In addition to the Data Protection Act 2018 and GDPR, practitioners need to balance the common law duty of confidence and the Human Rights Act 1998 against the effect on individuals or others of not sharing the information.

IT Systems are often a barrier to effective information sharing

No – IT systems, such as the Child Protection Information Sharing project (CP-IS), can be useful for information sharing. IT systems are most valuable when practitioners use the shared data to make more informed decisions about how to support and safeguard a child.

---

[14] Practitioners looking to share information should consider which processing condition in the Data Protection Act 2018 is most appropriate for use in the particular circumstances of the case. This may be the safeguarding processing condition or another relevant provision.

Statutory requirements for children in need

- under the Children Act 1989, local authorities are required to provide services for children in need for the purposes of safeguarding and promoting their welfare

- local authorities undertake assessments of the needs of individual children and must give due regard to a child's age and understanding when determining what, if any, services to provide. Every assessment must be informed by the views of the child as well as the family, and a child's wishes and feelings must be sought regarding the provision of services to be delivered. Where possible, children should be seen alone

- a child in need is defined under the Children Act 1989 as a child who is unlikely to achieve or maintain a reasonable level of health or development, or whose health and development is likely to be significantly or further impaired, without the provision of services; or a child who is disabled. Children in need may be assessed under section 17 of the Children Act 1989 by a social worker

- some children in need may require accommodation because there is no one who has parental responsibility for them, because they are lost or abandoned, or because the person who has been caring for them is prevented from providing them with suitable accommodation or care. Under section 20 of the Children Act 1989, the local authority has a duty to accommodate such children in need in their area

- when assessing children in need and providing services, specialist assessments may be required and, where possible, should be co-ordinated so that the child and family experience a coherent process and a single plan of action

- under section 47 of the Children Act 1989, where a local authority has reasonable cause to suspect that a child (who lives or is found in their area) is suffering or is likely to suffer significant harm, it has a duty to make such enquiries as it considers necessary to decide whether to take any action to safeguard or promote the child's welfare. Such enquiries, supported by other organisations and agencies, as appropriate, should be initiated where there are concerns about all forms of abuse, neglect. This includes female genital mutilation and other honour-based violence, and extra-familial threats including radicalisation and sexual or criminal exploitation

- there may be a need for immediate protection whilst an assessment or enquiries are carried out

Assessment of disabled children and their carers

28.   When undertaking an assessment of a disabled child, the local authority must also consider whether it is necessary to provide support under section 2 of the Chronically Sick and Disabled Persons Act (CSDPA) 1970[15]. Where a local authority is satisfied that the identified services and assistance can be provided under section 2 of the CSDPA, and it is necessary in order to meet a disabled child's needs, it must arrange to provide that support. Where a local authority is assessing the needs of a disabled child, a carer of that child may also require the local authority to undertake an assessment of their ability to provide, or to continue to provide, care for the child, under section 1 of the Carers (Recognition and Services) Act 1995. The local authority must take account of the results of any such assessment when deciding whether to provide services to the disabled child.

29.   If a local authority considers that a parent carer of a disabled child (see glossary) may have support needs, it must carry out an assessment under section 17ZD of the Children Act 1989. The local authority must also carry out such an assessment if a parent carer requests one. Such an assessment must consider whether it is appropriate for the parent carer to provide, or continue to provide, care for the disabled child, in light of the parent carer's needs and wishes.

Assessment of young carers

30.   If a local authority considers that a young carer (see glossary) may have support needs, it must carry out an assessment under section 17ZA of the Children Act 1989. The local authority must also carry out such an assessment if a young carer, or the parent of a young carer, requests one. Such an assessment must consider whether it is appropriate or excessive for the young carer to provide care for the person in question, in light of the young carer's needs and wishes. The Young Carers' (Needs Assessment) Regulations 2015[16] require local authorities to look at the needs of the whole family when carrying out a young carer's needs assessment. Young carers' assessments can be combined with assessments of adults in the household, with the agreement of the young carer and adults concerned.

Assessment of children in secure youth establishments

31.   Any assessment of children in secure youth establishments should take account of their specific needs. In all cases, the local authority in which a secure youth establishment is located is responsible for the safety and welfare of the children in that establishment. The host local authority should work with the governor, director, manager or principal of

---

[15] Chronically Sick and Disabled Persons Act (CSDPA) 1970.
[16] The Young Carers' (Need Assessment) Regulations 2015.

the secure youth establishment and the child's home local authority, their relevant Youth Offending Team and, where appropriate, the Youth Custody Service[17] to ensure that the child has a single, comprehensive support plan.

32. Where a child becomes looked-after, as a result of being remanded to youth detention accommodation (YDA), the local authority must visit the child and assess the child's needs before taking a decision. This information must be used to prepare a Detention Placement Plan (DPP), which must set out how the YDA and other practitioners will meet the child's needs whilst the child remains remanded. The DPP must be reviewed in the same way as a care plan for any other looked-after child[18].

Contextual safeguarding

33. As well as threats to the welfare of children from within their families, children may be vulnerable to abuse or exploitation from outside their families. These extra-familial threats might arise at school and other educational establishments, from within peer groups, or more widely from within the wider community and/or online. These threats can take a variety of different forms and children can be vulnerable to multiple threats, including: exploitation by criminal gangs and organised crime groups such as county lines; trafficking, online abuse; sexual exploitation and the influences of extremism leading to radicalisation. Extremist groups make use of the internet to radicalise and recruit and to promote extremist materials. Any potential harmful effects to individuals identified as vulnerable to extremist ideologies or being drawn into terrorism should also be considered[19].

34. Assessments of children in such cases should consider whether wider environmental factors are present in a child's life and are a threat to their safety and/or welfare. Children who may be alleged perpetrators should also be assessed to understand the impact of contextual issues on their safety and welfare. Interventions should focus on addressing these wider environmental factors, which are likely to be a threat to the safety and welfare of a number of different children who may or may not be known to local authority children's social care. Assessments of children in such cases should consider the individual needs and vulnerabilities of each child. They should look at the parental capacity to support the child, including helping the parents and carers to understand any risks and support them to keep children safe and assess potential risk to child.

---

[17] As the placing authority.
[18] Following the Legal Aid Sentencing and Punishment of Offenders Act 2012 all children and young people remanded by a court in criminal proceedings will be looked-after.
[19] Under the Counter-Terrorism and Security Act 2015.

35. Channel panels, established under the Counter-Terrorism and Security Act 2015, assess the extent to which identified individuals are vulnerable to being drawn into terrorism, and, where appropriate, arrange for support to be provided[20]. When assessing Channel referrals, local authorities and their partners should consider how best to align these with assessments undertaken under the Children Act 1989.

36. The Children Act 1989 promotes the view that all children and their parents should be considered as individuals and that family structures, culture, religion, ethnic origins and other characteristics should be respected. Local authorities should ensure they support and promote fundamental British values, of democracy, the rule of law, individual liberty, and mutual respect and tolerance of those with different faiths and beliefs.

37. The Counter-Terrorism and Security Act 2015 contains a duty on specified authorities in England, Wales and Scotland to have due regard to the need to prevent people from being drawn into terrorism.

Purpose of assessment

38. Whatever legislation the child is assessed under, the purpose of the assessment is always:

- to gather important information about a child and family
- to analyse their needs and/or the nature and level of any risk and harm being suffered by the child
- to decide whether the child is a child in need (section 17) or is suffering or likely to suffer significant harm (section 47)
- to provide support to address those needs to improve the child's outcomes and welfare and where necessary to make them safe

Local protocols for assessment

39. Local authorities, with their partners, should develop and publish local protocols for assessment. A local protocol should set out clear arrangements for how cases will be managed once a child is referred into local authority children's social care and be consistent with the requirements of this statutory guidance. The detail of each protocol will be led by the local authority in discussion and agreement with the safeguarding partners and relevant agencies where appropriate.

---

[20] Channel guidance.

40.   The local authority is publicly accountable for this protocol and all organisations and agencies have a responsibility to understand their local protocol.

41.   The local protocol should reflect where assessments for some children will require particular care. This is especially so for young carers, children with special educational needs (including to inform and be informed by Education, Health and Care Plans), unborn children where there are concerns, children in hospital, children with specific communication needs, asylum seeking children, children considered at risk of gang activity and association with organised crime groups, children at risk of female genital mutilation, children who are in the youth justice system, and children returning home.

42.   Where a child has other assessments, it is important that these are co-ordinated so that the child does not become lost between the different organisational procedures. There should be clear procedures for how these organisations and agencies will communicate with the child and family, and the local protocol for assessment should clarify how organisations and agencies and practitioners undertaking assessments and providing services can make contributions.

43.   The local protocol for assessment should set out the process for challenge by children and families by publishing the complaints procedures[21].

The principles and parameters of a good assessment

44.   Assessment should be a dynamic process, which analyses and responds to the changing nature and level of need and/or risk faced by the child from within and outside their family. It is important that the impact of what is happening to a child is clearly identified and that information is gathered, recorded and checked systematically, and discussed with the child and their parents/carers where appropriate.

45.   Any provision identified as being necessary through the assessment process should, if the local authority decides to provide such services, be provided without delay. A good assessment will monitor and record the impact of any services delivered to the child and family and review the help being delivered. Whilst services may be delivered to a parent or carer, the assessment should be focused on the needs of the child and on the impact any services are having on the child[22].

46.   Good assessments support practitioners to understand whether a child has needs relating to their care or a disability and/or is suffering or likely to suffer significant harm.

---

[21] Including as specified under Section 26(3) of the Children Act 1989 and the Children Act 1989 Representations Procedure (England) Regulations 2006.
[22] An assessment of the support needs of parent carers, or non-parent carers, of disabled children may be required.

The specific needs of disabled children and young carers should be given sufficient recognition and priority in the assessment process[23].

47.   The local authority should act decisively to protect the child from abuse and neglect including initiating care proceedings where existing interventions are insufficient[24]. Where an assessment in these circumstances identifies concerns but care proceedings are not initiated, the assessment should provide a valuable platform for ongoing engagement with the child and their family.

48.   Where a child becomes looked-after, the assessment will be the baseline for work with the family. Any needs that have been identified should be addressed before decisions are made about the child's return home. Assessment by a social worker is required before a looked after child under a care order returns home[25]. This will provide evidence of whether the necessary improvements have been made to ensure the child's safety when they return home. Following an assessment, appropriate support should be provided for children returning home, including where that return home is unplanned, to ensure that children continue to be adequately safeguarded.

49.   In order to carry out good assessments, social workers should have the relevant knowledge and skills set out in the Knowledge and Skills Statements for child and family social work[26].

50.   Social workers should have time to complete assessments and have access to high quality practice supervision. Principal social workers should support social workers, the local authority and partners to develop their assessment practice and decision making skills, and the practice methodology that underpins this.

51.   High quality assessments:

- are child-centred. Where there is a conflict of interest, decisions should be made in the child's best interests: be rooted in child development: be age-appropriate; and be informed by evidence

- are focused on action and outcomes for children

- are holistic in approach, addressing the child's needs within their family and any risks the child faces from within the wider community

- ensure equality of opportunity

---

[23] Recognised, valued and supported: Next steps for the Carers Strategy (2010).
[24] Further information about processes relating to care and court proceedings (including pre-proceedings) can be found in the statutory guidance document for local authorities, Court Orders and Pre-Proceedings (DfE, 2014).
[25] Under the Care Planning, Placement and Case Review (England) Regulations 2010.
[26] Knowledge and skills statements for child and family social work.

- involve children, ensuring that their voice is heard and provide appropriate support to enable this where the child has specific communication needs

- involve families

- identify risks to the safety and welfare of children

- build on strengths as well as identifying difficulties

- are integrated in approach

- are multi-agency and multi-disciplinary

- are a continuing process, not an event

- lead to action, including the provision of services

- review services provided on an ongoing basis

- are transparent and open to challenge

52.   Research has shown that taking a systematic approach to enquiries using a conceptual model is the best way to deliver a comprehensive assessment for all children. An example of such a model is set out in the diagram on the next page. It investigates three domains:

- the child's developmental needs, including whether they are suffering or likely to suffer significant harm

- the capacity of parents or carers (resident and non-resident) and any other adults living in the household to respond to those needs [27, 28]

- the impact and influence of wider family and any other adults living in the household as well as community and environmental circumstances

---

[27] An assessment of the support needs of parent carers of disabled children may be required.
[28] See Chapter 2 paragraph 30 on adults with parental responsibility for disabled children.

Assessment Framework

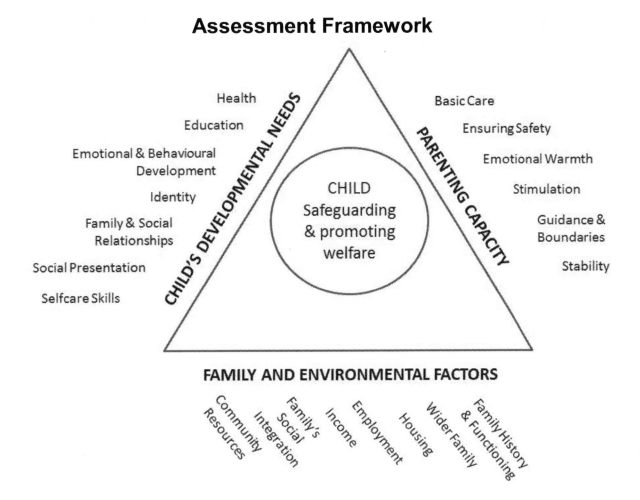

Focusing on the needs and views of the child

53.   Every assessment should reflect the unique characteristics of the child within their family and community context. Each child whose referral has been accepted by children's social care should have their individual needs assessed, including an analysis of the parental capacity to meet those needs whether they arise from issues within the family or the wider community. Frequently, more than one child from the same family is referred and siblings within the family should always be considered. Family assessments that include all members of the family should always ensure that the needs of individual children are distinct considerations.

54.   Where the child has links to a foreign country[29], a social worker may also need to work with colleagues abroad[30].

---

[29] A child with links to a foreign country may be a foreign national child, a child with dual nationality or a British child of foreign parents/national origin.

[30] Further guidance can be found in Working with foreign authorities: child protection and care orders (2014).

55.   Every assessment, including young carer, parent carer and non-parent carer assessments, should draw together relevant information gathered from the child and their family and from relevant practitioners including teachers and school staff, early years workers, health practitioners, the police and adult social care. Where a child has been looked-after and has returned home, information from previous assessments and case records should also be reviewed.

Developing a clear analysis

56.   The social worker should analyse all the information gathered from the assessment, including from a young carer's, parent carer's or non-parent carer's assessment, to decide the nature and level of the child's needs and the level of risk, if any, they may be facing. The social worker should receive insight and challenge to their emerging hypothesis from their practice supervisors and other relevant practitioners who should challenge the social worker's assumptions as part of this process. An informed decision should be taken on the nature of any action required and which services should be provided. Social workers, their managers and other practitioners should be mindful of the requirement to understand the level of need and risk in, or faced by, a family from the child's perspective and plan accordingly, understanding both protective and risk factors the child is facing. The analysis should inform the action to be taken which will have maximum impact on the child's welfare and outcomes.

57.   No system can fully eliminate risk. Understanding risk involves judgment and balance. To manage risks, social workers and other practitioners should make decisions with the best interests of the child in mind, informed by the evidence available and underpinned by knowledge of child development.

58.   Critical reflection through supervision should strengthen the analysis in each assessment.

59.   A desire to think the best of adults and to hope they can overcome their difficulties should not subvert the need to protect children from chaotic, abusive and neglectful homes. Social workers and practice supervisors should always reflect the latest research on the impact of abuse and neglect and relevant findings from serious case and practice reviews when analysing the level of need and risk faced by the child. This should be reflected in the case recording.

60.   Assessment is a dynamic and continuous process that should build upon the history of every individual case, responding to the impact of any previous services and analysing what further action might be needed. Social workers should build on this with help from other practitioners from the moment that a need is identified. A high quality

assessment is one in which evidence is built and revised throughout the process and takes account of family history and the child's experience of cumulative abuse.

61.   A social worker may arrive at a judgment early in the case but this may need to be revised as the case progresses and further information comes to light. It is a characteristic of skilled practice that social workers revisit their assumptions in the light of new evidence and take action to revise their decisions in the best interests of the individual child.

62.   Decision points and review points involving the child and family and relevant practitioners should be used to keep the assessment on track. This is to ensure that help is given in a timely and appropriate way and that the impact of this help is analysed and evaluated in terms of the improved outcomes and welfare of the child.

Focusing on outcomes

63.   Every assessment should be focused on outcomes, deciding which services and support to provide to deliver improved welfare for the child.

64.   Where the outcome of the assessment is continued local authority children's social care involvement, the social worker should agree a plan of action with other practitioners and discuss this with the child and their family. The plan should set out what services are to be delivered, and what actions are to be undertaken, by whom and for what purpose.

65.   Many services provided will be for parents or carers (and may include services identified in a parent carer's or non-parent carer's needs assessment)[31]. The plan should reflect this and set clear measurable outcomes for the child and expectations for the parents, with measurable, reviewable actions for them.

66.   The plan should be reviewed regularly to analyse whether sufficient progress has been made to meet the child's needs and the level of risk faced by the child. This will be important for neglect cases where parents and carers can make small improvements. The test should be whether any improvements in adult behaviour are sufficient and sustained. Social workers should consider the need for further action and record their decisions. The review points should be agreed by the social worker with other practitioners and with the child and family to continue evaluating the impact of any change on the welfare of the child.

67.   Effective practitioner supervision can play a critical role in ensuring a clear focus on a child's welfare. Supervision should support practitioners to reflect critically on the impact of their decisions on the child and their family. The social worker should review the plan

---

[31] Section 17ZD of the Children Act 1989 and section 1 of the Carers (Recognition and Services) Act 1995.

for the child. They should ask whether the help given is leading to a significant positive change for the child and whether the pace of that change is appropriate for the child. Practitioners working with children should always have access to colleagues to talk through their concerns and judgments affecting the welfare of the child. Assessment should remain an ongoing process, with the impact of services informing future decisions about action.

68.   Known transition points for the child should be planned for in advance. This includes where children are likely to transition between child and adult services.

Timeliness

69.   The timeliness of an assessment is a critical element of the quality of that assessment and the outcomes for the child. The speed with which an assessment is carried out after a child's case has been referred into local authority children's social care should be determined by the needs of the individual child and the nature and level of any risk of harm they face. This will require judgments to be made by the social worker on each individual case. Adult assessments, for example, parent carer or non-parent carer assessments, should also be carried out in a timely manner, consistent with the needs of the child.

70.   Once the referral has been accepted by local authority children's social care, the lead practitioner role falls to a social worker. The social worker should clarify with the referrer, when known, the nature of the concerns and how and why they have arisen.

71.   Within **one working day** of a referral being received, a local authority social worker should acknowledge receipt to the referrer and **make a decision** about next steps and the type of response required. This will include determining whether:

- ☐ the child requires immediate protection and urgent action is required
- ☐ the child is in need and should be assessed under section 17 of the Children Act 1989
- ☐ there is reasonable cause to suspect that the child is suffering or likely to suffer significant harm, and whether enquires must be made and the child assessed under section 47 of the Children Act 1989
- ☐ any services are required by the child and family and what type of services
- ☐ further specialist assessments are required to help the local authority to decide what further action to take
- ☐ to see the child as soon as possible if the decision is taken that the referral requires further assessment

72.   Where requested to do so by local authority children's social care, practitioners from other parts of the local authority such as housing and those in health organisations have a duty to co-operate under section 27 of the Children Act 1989 by assisting the local authority in carrying out its children's social care functions.

73.   The child and family must be informed of the action to be taken, unless a decision is taken on the basis that this may jeopardise a police investigation or place the child at risk of significant harm.

74.   For children who are in need of immediate protection, action must be taken by the social worker, or the police or the NSPCC[32] if removal is required, as soon as possible after the referral has been made to local authority children's social care (sections 44 and 46 of the Children Act 1989).

75.   The maximum timeframe for the assessment to conclude, such that it is possible to reach a decision on next steps, should be no longer than 45 working days from the point of referral. If, in discussion with a child and their family and other practitioners, an assessment exceeds 45 working days, the social worker should record the reasons for exceeding the time limit.

76.   Whatever the timescale for assessment, where particular needs are identified at any stage of the assessment, social workers should not wait until the assessment reaches a conclusion before commissioning services to support the child and their family. In some cases, the needs of the child will mean that a quick assessment will be required.

77.   It is the responsibility of the social worker to make clear to children and families how the assessment will be carried out and when they can expect a decision on next steps. Local authorities should determine their local assessment processes through a local protocol.

Processes for managing individual cases

78.   The following descriptors and flow charts set out the steps that practitioners should take when working together to assess and provide services for children who may be in need, including those suffering harm. The flow charts cover:

- the referral process into local authority children's social care

- immediate protection for children at risk of significant harm

- the process for determining next steps for a child who has been assessed as being 'in need'

---

[32] National Society for the Prevention of Cruelty to Children.

☐ the processes for children where there is reasonable cause to suspect that the child is suffering or likely to suffer significant harm (this includes immediate protection for children at serious risk of harm)

Flow chart 1: Action taken when a child is referred to local authority children's social care services

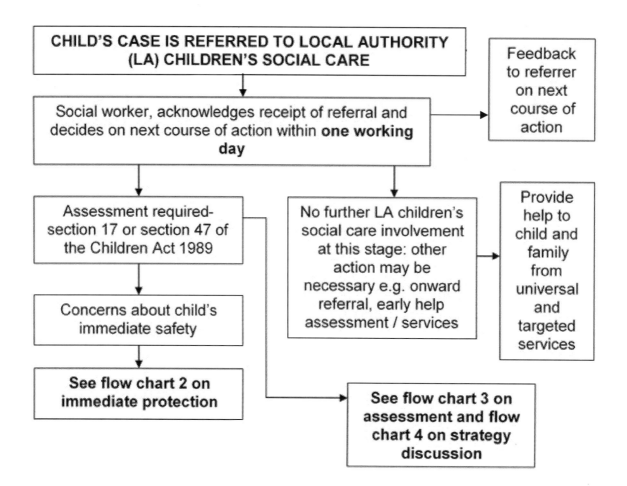

Immediate Protection

Where there is a risk to the life of a child or a likelihood of serious immediate harm, local authority social workers, the police or NSPCC should use their statutory child protection powers to **act immediately to secure the safety of the child**.

If it is necessary to remove a child from their home, a local authority must, wherever possible and unless a child's safety is otherwise at immediate risk, apply for an **Emergency Protection Order (EPO)**. Police powers to remove a child in an emergency should be used only in exceptional circumstances where there is insufficient time to seek an EPO or for reasons relating to the immediate safety of the child.

An **EPO**, made by the court, gives authority to remove a child and places them under the protection of the applicant.

When considering whether emergency action is necessary, an agency should always consider the needs of other children in the same household or in the household of an alleged perpetrator.

The **local authority** in whose area a child is found in circumstances that require emergency action (the first authority) is responsible for taking emergency action.

If the child is looked-after by, or the subject of a child protection plan in another authority, the first authority must consult the authority responsible for the child. Only when the second local authority explicitly accepts responsibility (to be followed up in writing) is the first authority relieved of its responsibility to take emergency action.

Multi-agency working

Planned emergency action will normally take place following an immediate strategy discussion. Social workers, the police or NSPCC should:

- initiate a strategy discussion to discuss planned emergency action. Where a single agency has to act immediately, a strategy discussion should take place as soon as possible after action has been taken

- see the child (this should be done by a practitioner from the agency taking the emergency action) to decide how best to protect them and whether to seek an EPO

- wherever possible, obtain legal advice before initiating legal action, in particular when an EPO is being sought

Related information: For further guidance on EPOs see Chapter 4 of *the statutory guidance document for local authorities,* Court orders and pre-proceedings (DfE, April 2014).

Flow chart 2: Immediate protection

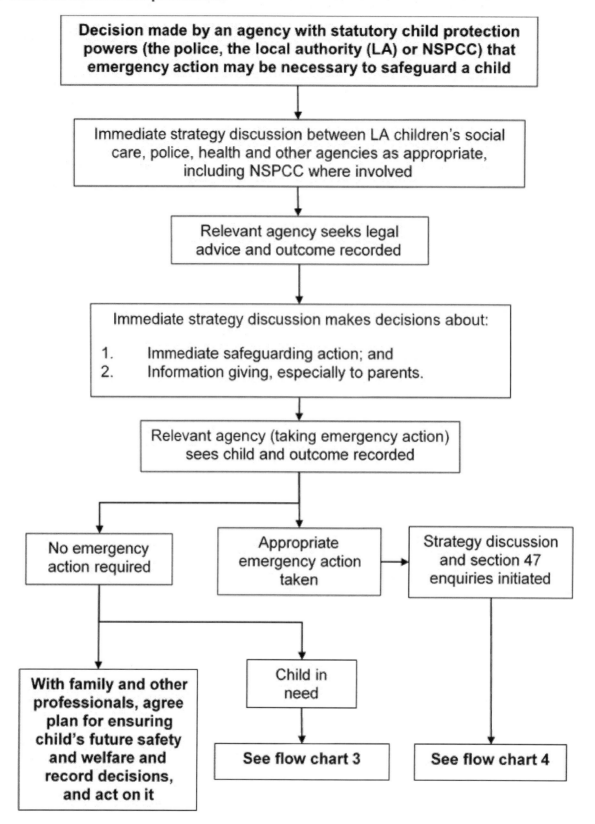

Decision made by an agency with statutory child protection powers (the police, the local authority (LA) or NSPCC) that emergency action may be necessary to safeguard a child

Immediate strategy discussion between LA children's social care, police, health and other agencies as appropriate, including NSPCC where involved

Relevant agency seeks legal advice and outcome recorded

Immediate strategy discussion makes decisions about:

1.   Immediate safeguarding action; and
2.   Information giving, especially to parents.

Relevant agency (taking emergency action) sees child and outcome recorded

No emergency action required

Appropriate emergency action taken

Strategy discussion and section 47 enquiries initiated

With family and other professionals, agree plan for ensuring child's future safety and welfare and record decisions, and act on it

Child in need

See flow chart 3

See flow chart 4

Assessment of a child under the Children Act 1989

Following acceptance of a referral by the local authority children's social care, a social worker should lead a multi-agency assessment under section 17 of the Children Act 1989. Local authorities have a duty to ascertain the child's wishes and feelings and take account of them when planning the provision of services. Assessments should be carried out in a timely manner reflecting the needs of the individual child, as set out in this chapter.

Where the local authority children's social care decides to provide services, a multi-agency child in need plan should be developed which sets out which organisations and agencies will provide which services to the child and family. The plan should set clear measurable outcomes for the child and expectations for the parents. The plan should reflect the positive aspects of the family situation as well as the weaknesses.

Where a child in need has moved permanently to another local authority area, the original authority should ensure that all relevant information (including the child in need plan) is shared with the receiving local authority as soon as possible. The receiving local authority should consider whether support services are still required and discuss with the child and family what might be needed, based on a timely re-assessment of the child's needs, as set out in this chapter. Support should continue to be provided by the original local authority in the intervening period. The receiving authority should work with the original authority to ensure that any changes to the services and support provided are managed carefully.

Where a child in need is approaching 18 years of age, this transition point should be planned for in advance. This includes where children are likely to transition between child and adult services.

Where information gathered during an assessment (which may be very brief) results in the social worker suspecting that the child is suffering or likely to suffer significant harm, the local authority should hold a strategy discussion to enable it to decide, with other agencies, whether it must initiate enquiries under section 47 of the Children Act 1989.

Purpose:	Assessments should determine whether the child is in need, the nature of any services required and whether any specialist assessments should be undertaken to assist the local authority in its decision-making.

Assessment of a child under the Children Act 1989

Social workers should:	• lead on an assessment and complete it in line with the locally agreed protocol according to the child's needs and within 45 working days from the point of referral into local authority children's social care
	• see the child within a timescale that is appropriate to the nature of the concerns expressed at referral, according to an agreed plan
	• conduct interviews with the child and family members, separately and together as appropriate. Initial discussions with the child should be conducted in a way that minimises distress to them and maximises the likelihood that they will provide accurate and complete information, avoiding leading or suggestive questions
	• record the assessment findings and decisions and next steps following the assessment
	• inform, in writing, all the relevant agencies and the family of their decisions and, if the child is a child in need, of the plan for providing support
	• inform the referrer of what action has been or will be taken
The police should:	• assist other organisations and agencies to carry out their responsibilities where there are concerns about the child's welfare, whether or not a crime has been committed. If a crime has been committed, the police should be informed by the local authority children's social care
All involved practitioners should:	• be involved in the assessment and provide further information about the child and family
	• agree further action including what services would help the child and family and inform local authority children's social care if any immediate action is required
	• seek advice and guidance as required and in line with local practice guidance

Flow chart 3: Action taken for an assessment of a child under the Children Act 1989

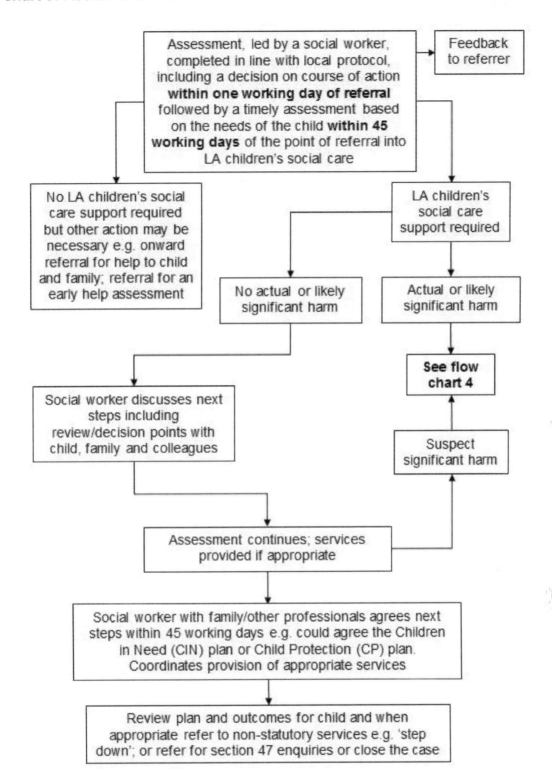

Assessment, led by a social worker, completed in line with local protocol, including a decision on course of action **within one working day of referral** followed by a timely assessment based on the needs of the child **within 45 working days** of the point of referral into LA children's social care

Feedback to referrer

No LA children's social care support required but other action may be necessary e.g. onward referral for help to child and family; referral for an early help assessment

LA children's social care support required

No actual or likely significant harm

Actual or likely significant harm

See flow chart 4

Social worker discusses next steps including review/decision points with child, family and colleagues

Suspect significant harm

Assessment continues; services provided if appropriate

Social worker with family/other professionals agrees next steps within 45 working days e.g. could agree the Children in Need (CIN) plan or Child Protection (CP) plan. Coordinates provision of appropriate services

Review plan and outcomes for child and when appropriate refer to non-statutory services e.g. 'step down'; or refer for section 47 enquiries or close the case

Strategy discussion

Whenever there is reasonable cause to suspect that a child is suffering or is likely to suffer significant harm there should be a strategy discussion involving local authority children's social care (including the residential or fostering service, if the child is looked-after), the police, health and other bodies such as the referring agency. This might take the form of a multi-agency meeting or phone calls and more than one discussion may be necessary. A strategy discussion can take place following a referral or at any other time, including during the assessment process and when new information is received on an already open case.

Purpose:	Local authority children's social care should convene a strategy discussion to determine the child's welfare and plan rapid future action if there is reasonable cause to suspect the child is suffering or is likely to suffer significant harm.
Strategy discussion attendees:	A local authority social worker, health practitioners and a police representative should, as a minimum, be involved in the strategy discussion. Other relevant practitioners will depend on the nature of the individual case but may include: • the practitioner or agency which made the referral • the child's school or nursery • any health or care services the child or family members are receiving All attendees should be sufficiently senior to make decisions on behalf of their organisation and agencies.

Strategy discussion

Strategy discussion tasks:	The discussion should be used to: • share available information • agree the conduct and timing of any criminal investigation • decide whether enquiries under section 47 of the Children Act 1989 must be undertaken Where there are grounds to initiate an enquiry under section 47 of the Children Act 1989, decisions should be made as to: • what further information is needed if an assessment is already underway and how it will be obtained and recorded • what immediate and short term action is required to support the child, and who will do what by when • whether legal action is required The timescale for the assessment to reach a decision on next steps should be based upon the needs of the individual child, consistent with the local protocol and no longer than **45 working days** from the point of referral into local authority children's social care. The principles and parameters for the assessment of children in need at chapter 1 paragraph 40 should be followed for assessments undertaken under section 47 of the Children Act 1989.
Social workers should:	Convene the strategy discussion and make sure it: • considers the child's welfare and safety, and identifies the level of risk faced by the child • decides what information should be shared with the child and family (on the basis that information is not shared if this may jeopardise a police investigation or place the child at risk of significant harm) • agrees what further action is required, and who will do what by when, where an EPO is in place or the child is the subject of police powers of protection • records agreed decisions in accordance with local recording procedures • follows up actions to make sure what was agreed gets done

Strategy discussion

Health practitioners should:	<ul><li>advise about the appropriateness or otherwise of medical assessments, and explain the benefits that arise from assessing previously unmanaged health matters that may be further evidence of neglect or maltreatment</li><li>provide and co-ordinate any specific information from relevant practitioners regarding family health, maternity health, school health mental health, domestic abuse and violence and substance misuse to assist strategy and decision making</li><li>secure additional expert advice and support from named and/or designated professionals for more complex cases following preliminary strategy discussions</li><li>undertake appropriate examinations or observations, and further investigations or tests, to determine how the child's health or development may be impaired</li></ul>
The police should:	<ul><li>discuss the basis for any criminal investigation and any relevant processes that other organisations and agencies might need to know about, including the timing and methods of evidence gathering</li><li>lead the criminal investigation (local authority children's social care have the lead for the section 47 enquires and assessment of the child's welfare) where joint enquiries take place</li></ul>

Flow chart 4: Action following a strategy discussion

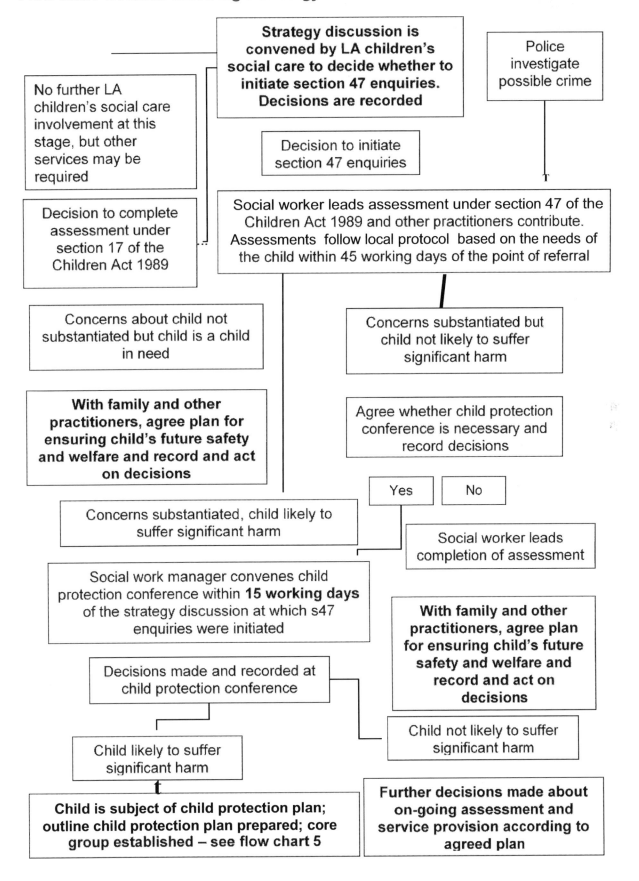

Strategy discussion is convened by LA children's social care to decide whether to initiate section 47 enquiries. Decisions are recorded

Police investigate possible crime

No further LA children's social care involvement at this stage, but other services may be required

Decision to initiate section 47 enquiries

Decision to complete assessment under section 17 of the Children Act 1989

Social worker leads assessment under section 47 of the Children Act 1989 and other practitioners contribute. Assessments follow local protocol based on the needs of the child within 45 working days of the point of referral

Concerns about child not substantiated but child is a child in need

Concerns substantiated but child not likely to suffer significant harm

With family and other practitioners, agree plan for ensuring child's future safety and welfare and record and act on decisions

Agree whether child protection conference is necessary and record decisions

Yes | No

Concerns substantiated, child likely to suffer significant harm

Social worker leads completion of assessment

Social work manager convenes child protection conference within **15 working days** of the strategy discussion at which s47 enquiries were initiated

With family and other practitioners, agree plan for ensuring child's future safety and welfare and record and act on decisions

Decisions made and recorded at child protection conference

Child not likely to suffer significant harm

Child likely to suffer significant harm

Child is subject of child protection plan; outline child protection plan prepared; core group established – see flow chart 5

Further decisions made about on-going assessment and service provision according to agreed plan

Initiating section 47 enquiries

A section 47 enquiry is carried out by undertaking or continuing with an assessment in accordance with the guidance set out in this chapter and following the principles and parameters of a good assessment.

Local authority social workers should lead assessments under section 47 of the Children Act 1989. The police, health practitioners, teachers and school staff and other relevant practitioners should help the local authority in undertaking its enquiries.

Purpose:	A section 47 enquiry is initiated to decide whether and what type of action is required to safeguard and promote the welfare of a child who is suspected of or likely to be suffering significant harm.
Social workers should:	<ul><li>lead the assessment in accordance with this guidance</li><li>carry out enquiries in a way that minimises distress for the child and family</li><li>see the child who is the subject of concern to ascertain their wishes and feelings; assess their understanding of their situation; assess their relationships and circumstances more broadly</li><li>interview parents/carers and determine the wider social and environmental factors that might impact on them and their child</li><li>systematically gather information about the child's and family's history</li><li>analyse the findings of the assessment and evidence about what interventions are likely to be most effective with other relevant practitioners.</li><li>determine the child's needs and the level of risk of harm faced by the child to inform what help should be provided and act to provide that help</li><li>follow the guidance set out in 'Achieving Best Evidence in Criminal Proceedings: Guidance on interviewing victims and witnesses, and guidance on using special measures', where a decision has been made to undertake a joint interview of the child as part of any criminal investigation[33]</li></ul>

---

[33] Ministry of Justice Achieving Best Evidence in Criminal Proceedings: Guidance on interviewing victims and witnesses, and guidance on using special measures (2011).

Initiating section 47 enquiries

The police should:	• help other organisations and agencies understand the reasons for concerns about the child's safety and welfare • decide whether or not police investigations reveal grounds for instigating criminal proceedings • make available to other practitioners any evidence gathered to inform discussions about the child's welfare • follow the guidance set out in 'Achieving Best Evidence in Criminal Proceedings: Guidance' on interviewing victims and witnesses, and guidance on using special measures, where a decision has been made to undertake a joint interview of the child as part of the criminal investigations
Health practitioners should:	• provide any of a range of specialist assessments. For example, paediatric or forensic medical assessments, physiotherapists, occupational therapists, speech and language therapists and/or child psychologists may be involved in specific assessments relating to the child's developmental progress. The lead health practitioner (probably a consultant paediatrician, or possibly the child's GP) may need to request and co-ordinate these assessments • ensure appropriate treatment and follow up health concerns, such as administration of missing vaccines
All involved practitioners should:	• contribute to the assessment as required, providing information about the child and family • consider whether a joint enquiry/investigation team may need to speak to a child victim without the knowledge of the parent/carers • seek advice and guidance as required and in line with local practice guidance

Outcome of section 47 enquiries

Local authority social workers are responsible for deciding what action to take and how to proceed following section 47 enquiries.

If local authority children's social care decides not to proceed with a child protection conference then other practitioners involved with the child and family have the right to request that local authority children's social care convene a conference if they have serious concerns that a child's welfare may not be adequately safeguarded. As a last resort, the safeguarding partners should have in place a quick and straightforward means of resolving differences of opinion.

Where concerns of significant harm are not substantiated:

Social workers should:	<ul><li>discuss the case with the child, parents and other practitioners</li><li>determine whether support from any services may be helpful and help secure it</li><li>consider whether the child's health and development should be re-assessed regularly against specific objectives and decide who has responsibility for doing this</li></ul>
All involved practitioners should:	<ul><li>participate in further discussions as necessary</li><li>contribute to the development of any plan as appropriate</li><li>provide services as specified in the plan for the child</li><li>review the impact of services delivered as agreed in the plan</li><li>seek advice and guidance as required and in line with local practice guidance</li></ul>

Where concerns of significant harm are substantiated and the child is judged to be suffering or likely to suffer significant harm:	
Social workers should:	• convene an initial child protection conference (see next section for details). The timing of this conference should depend on the urgency of the case and respond to the needs of the child and the nature and severity of the harm they may be facing. The initial child protection conference should take place within 15 working days of a strategy discussion, or the strategy discussion at which section 47 enquiries were initiated if more than one has been held • consider whether any practitioners with specialist knowledge should be invited to participate • ensure that the child and their parents understand the purpose of the conference and who will attend • help prepare the child if they are attending or making representations through a third party to the conference. Give information about advocacy agencies and explain that the family may bring an advocate, friend or supporter
All involved practitioners should:	• contribute to the information their agency provides ahead of the conference, setting out the nature of the organisation's or agency's involvement with the child and family • consider, in conjunction with the police and the appointed conference Chair, whether the report can and should be shared with the parents and if so when • attend the conference and take part in decision making when invited • seek advice and guidance as required and in line with local practice guidance

Initial child protection conferences

Following section 47 enquiries, an initial child protection conference brings together family members (and the child where appropriate), with the supporters, advocates and practitioners most involved with the child and family, to make decisions about the child's future safety, health and development. If concerns relate to an unborn child, consideration should be given as to whether to hold a child protection conference prior to the child's birth.

Purpose:	To bring together and analyse, in an inter-agency setting, all relevant information and plan how best to safeguard and promote the welfare of the child. It is the responsibility of the conference to make recommendations on how organisations and agencies work together to safeguard the child in future. Conference tasks include: • appointing a lead statutory body (either local authority children's social care or NSPCC) and a lead social worker, who should be a qualified, experienced social worker and an employee of the lead statutory body • identifying membership of the core group of practitioners and family members who will develop and implement the child protection plan • establishing timescales for meetings of the core group, production of a child protection plan and for child protection review meetings • agreeing an outline child protection plan, with clear actions and timescales, including a clear sense of how much improvement is needed, by when, so that success can be judged clearly
The Conference Chair:	• is accountable to the Director of Children's Services. Where possible the same person should chair subsequent child protection reviews • should be a practitioner, independent of operational and/or line management responsibilities for the case • should meet the child and parents in advance to ensure they understand the purpose and the process
Social workers should:	• convene, attend and present information about the reason for the conference, their understanding of the child's needs, parental capacity and family and environmental context and evidence of how the child has been abused or neglected and its impact on their health and development

Initial child protection conferences

	• analyse the information to enable informed decisions about what action is necessary to safeguard and promote the welfare of the child who is the subject of the conference • share the conference information with the child and family beforehand (where appropriate) • prepare a report for the conference on the child and family which sets out and analyses what is known about the child and family and the local authority's recommendation • record conference decisions and recommendations and ensure action follows
All involved practitioners should:	• work together to safeguard the child from harm in the future, taking timely, effective action according to the plan agreed
Safeguarding partners should:	• monitor the effectiveness of these arrangements

The child protection plan

Actions and responsibilities following the initial child protection conference

Purpose:	The aim of the child protection plan is to: • ensure the child is safe from harm and prevent them from suffering further harm • promote the child's health and development • support the family and wider family members to safeguard and promote the welfare of their child, provided it is in the best interests of the child
Local authority children's social care should:	• designate a social worker to be the lead practitioner as they carry statutory responsibility for the child's welfare • consider the evidence and decide what legal action to take if any, where a child has suffered or is likely to suffer significant harm • define the local protocol for timeliness of circulating plans after the child protection conference
Social workers should:	• be the lead practitioner for inter-agency work with the child and family, co-ordinating the contribution of family members and practitioners into putting the child protection plan into effect • develop the outline child protection plan into a more detailed interagency plan and circulate to relevant practitioners (and family where appropriate) • ensure the child protection plan is aligned and integrated with any associated offender risk management plan • undertake direct work with the child and family in accordance with the child protection plan, taking into account the child's wishes and feelings and the views of the parents in so far as they are consistent with the child's welfare • complete the child's and family's in-depth assessment, securing contributions from core group members and others as necessary • explain the plan to the child in a manner which is in accordance with their age and understanding and agree the plan with the child • consider the need to inform the relevant Embassy if the child has links to a foreign country

The child protection plan

	• co-ordinate reviews of progress against the planned outcomes set out in the plan, updating as required. The first review should be held within three months of the initial conference and further reviews at intervals of no more than six months for as long as the child remains subject of a child protection plan
	• record decisions and actions agreed at core group meetings as well as the written views of those who were not able to attend, and follow up those actions to ensure they take place. The child protection plan should be updated as necessary
	• lead core group activity
The core group should:	• meet within 10 working days from the initial child protection conference if the child is the subject of a child protection plan
	• further develop the outline child protection plan, based on assessment findings, and set out what needs to change, by how much, and by when in order for the child to be safe and have their needs met
	• decide what steps need to be taken, and by whom, to complete the in-depth assessment to inform decisions about the child's safety and welfare
	• implement the child protection plan and take joint responsibility for carrying out the agreed tasks, monitoring progress and outcomes, and refining the plan as needed

Child protection review conference

The review conference procedures for preparation, decision-making and other procedures should be the same as those for an initial child protection conference.

Purpose:	To review whether the child is continuing to suffer or is likely to suffer significant harm, and review developmental progress against child protection plan outcomes. To consider whether the child protection plan should continue or should be changed.
Social workers should:	• attend and lead the organisation of the conference • determine when the review conference should be held within three months of the initial conference, and thereafter at maximum intervals of six months • provide information to enable informed decisions about what action is necessary to safeguard and promote the welfare of the child who is the subject of the child protection plan, and about the effectiveness and impact of action taken so far • share the conference information with the child and family beforehand, where appropriate • record conference outcomes • decide whether to initiate family court proceedings (all the children in the household should be considered, even if concerns are only expressed about one child) if the child is considered to be suffering significant harm
All involved practitioners should:	• attend, when invited, and provide details of their involvement with the child and family • produce reports for the child protection review. This information will provide an overview of work undertaken by family members and practitioners, and evaluate the impact on the child's welfare against the planned outcomes set out in the child protection plan.

Flow chart 5: What happens after the child protection conference, including the review?

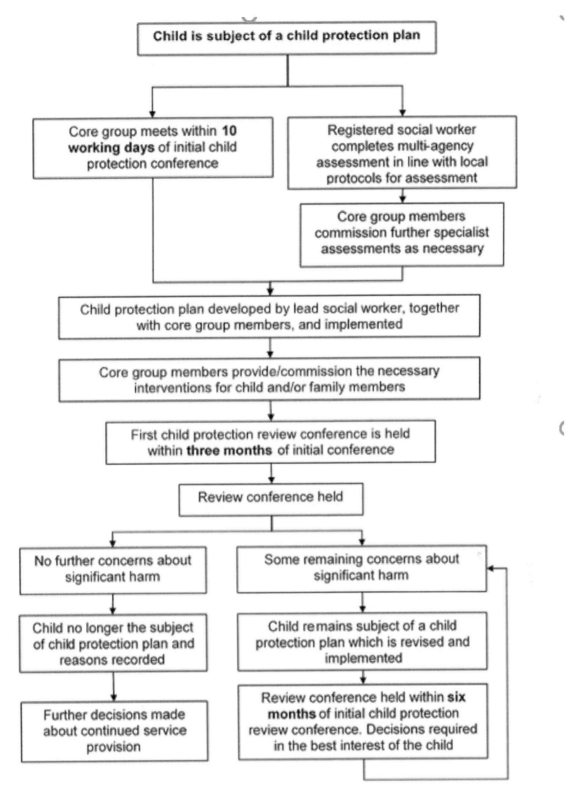

Discontinuing the Child Protection Plan

A child should no longer be the subject of a child protection plan if:

- it is judged that the child is no longer continuing to or is likely to suffer significant harm and therefore no longer requires safeguarding by means of a child protection plan

- the child and family have moved permanently to another local authority area. In such cases, the receiving local authority should convene a child protection conference within 15 working days of being notified of the move. Only after this event may the original local authority discontinue its child protection plan

- the child has reached 18 years of age (to end the child protection plan, the local authority should have a review around the child's birthday and this should be planned in advance), has died or has permanently left the United Kingdom

Social workers should:	<ul><li>notify, as a minimum, all agency representatives who were invited to attend the initial child protection conference that led to the plan</li><li>consider whether support services are still required and discuss with the child and family what might be needed, based on a re-assessment of the child's needs</li></ul>

Children returning home

Where the decision to return a child to the care of their family is planned, the local authority should undertake an assessment while the child is looked-after – as part of the care planning process (under regulation 39 of the Care Planning Regulations 2010). This assessment should consider what services and support the child (and their family) might need. The outcome of this assessment should be included in the child's care plan. The decision to cease to look after a child will, in most cases, require approval under regulation 39 of the Care Planning Regulations 2010.

Where a child who is accommodated under section 20 returns home in an unplanned way, for example, the decision is not made as part of the care planning process but the parent removes the child or the child decides to leave, the local authority must consider whether there are any immediate concerns about the safety and wellbeing of the child. If there are concerns about a child's safety the local authority should take appropriate action, including that the local authority must make enquiries under section 47 of the Children Act 1989 if there is concern that the child is suffering or likely to suffer significant harm.

There should be a clear plan for all children who return home that reflects current and previous assessments, focuses on outcomes and includes details of services and support required. Action to be taken following reunification:

- practitioners should make the timeline and decision making process for providing ongoing services and support clear to the child and family

- when reviewing outcomes, children should, wherever possible, be seen alone. Practitioners have a duty to ascertain their wishes and feelings regarding the provision of services being delivered

- the impact of services and support should be monitored and recorded, and where a child is remanded to local authority or youth detention accommodation, consideration must be given to what on-going support and accommodation the child may need after their period of remand[34]. This should be included in either their care plan or, if remanded to youth detention accommodation, detention placement plan.

---

[34] The Children Act 1989 Guidance and Regulations Volume 2: Care, planning, placement and case review paragraph 8.20.

Flow chart 6: Children returning home from care to their families

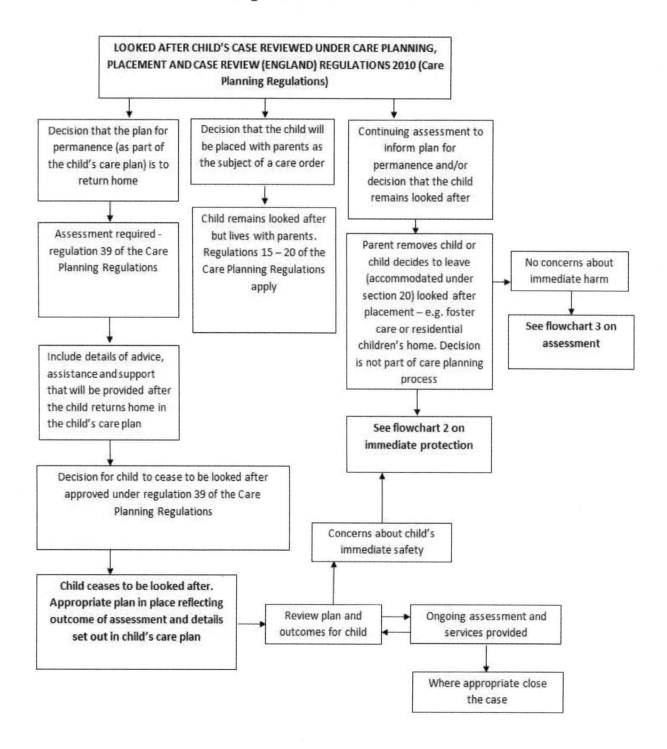

LOOKED AFTER CHILD'S CASE REVIEWED UNDER CARE PLANNING, PLACEMENT AND CASE REVIEW (ENGLAND) REGULATIONS 2010 (Care Planning Regulations)

Decision that the plan for permanence (as part of the child's care plan) is to return home

Decision that the child will be placed with parents as the subject of a care order

Continuing assessment to inform plan for permanence and/or decision that the child remains looked after

Assessment required - regulation 39 of the Care Planning Regulations

Child remains looked after but lives with parents. Regulations 15 – 20 of the Care Planning Regulations apply

Parent removes child or child decides to leave (accommodated under section 20) looked after placement – e.g. foster care or residential children's home. Decision is not part of care planning process

No concerns about immediate harm

See flowchart 3 on assessment

Include details of advice, assistance and support that will be provided after the child returns home in the child's care plan

See flowchart 2 on immediate protection

Decision for child to cease to be looked after approved under regulation 39 of the Care Planning Regulations

Concerns about child's immediate safety

Child ceases to be looked after. Appropriate plan in place reflecting outcome of assessment and details set out in child's care plan

Review plan and outcomes for child

Ongoing assessment and services provided

Where appropriate close the case

Chapter 2: Organisational responsibilities

1.   The previous chapter set out how organisations and agencies should take a co-ordinated approach to ensure children are effectively safeguarded. A range of individual organisations and agencies working with children and families have specific statutory duties to promote the welfare of children and ensure they are protected from harm. These duties, as applied to individual organisations and agencies, are set out in this chapter.

Section 11 of the Children Act 2004

Places duties on a range of organisations, agencies and individuals to ensure their functions, and any services that they contract out to others, are discharged having regard to the need to safeguard and promote the welfare of children.

---

2.   **Section 11** places a duty on:

- local authorities and district councils that provide children's and other types of services, including children's and adult social care services, public health, housing, sport, culture and leisure services, licensing authorities and youth services

- NHS organisations and agencies and the independent sector, including NHS England and clinical commissioning groups, NHS Trusts, NHS Foundation Trusts and General Practitioners

- the police, including police and crime commissioners and the chief officer of each police force in England and the Mayor's Office for Policing and Crime in London

- the British Transport Police

- the National Probation Service and Community Rehabilitation Companies[35]

- Governors/Directors of Prisons and Young Offender Institutions (YOIs)

- Directors of Secure Training Centres (STCs)

- Principals of Secure Colleges

- Youth Offending Teams/Services (YOTs)

3.   These organisations and agencies should have in place arrangements that reflect the importance of safeguarding and promoting the welfare of children, including:

- a clear line of accountability for the commissioning and/or provision of services designed to safeguard and promote the welfare of children

---

[35] The section 11 duty is conferred on the Community Rehabilitation Companies by virtue of contractual arrangements entered into with the Secretary of State.

- a senior board level lead with the required knowledge, skills and expertise or sufficiently qualified and experienced to take leadership responsibility for the organisation's/agency's safeguarding arrangements

- a culture of listening to children and taking account of their wishes and feelings, both in individual decisions and the development of services

- clear whistleblowing procedures, which reflect the principles in Sir Robert Francis' Freedom to Speak Up Review and are suitably referenced in staff training and codes of conduct, and a culture that enables issues about safeguarding and promoting the welfare of children to be addressed[36]

- clear escalation policies for staff to follow when their child safeguarding concerns are not being addressed within their organisation or by other agencies

- arrangements which set out clearly the processes for sharing information, with other practitioners and with safeguarding partners

- a designated practitioner (or, for health commissioning and health provider organisations/agencies, designated and named practitioners) for child safeguarding. Their role is to support other practitioners in their organisations and agencies to recognise the needs of children, including protection from possible abuse or neglect. Designated practitioner roles should always be explicitly defined in job descriptions. Practitioners should be given sufficient time, funding, supervision and support to fulfil their child welfare and safeguarding responsibilities effectively

- safe recruitment practices and ongoing safe working practices for individuals whom the organisation or agency permit to work regularly with children, including policies on when to obtain a criminal record check

- appropriate supervision and support for staff, including undertaking safeguarding training

- creating a culture of safety, equality and protection within the services they provide

In addition:

- employers are responsible for ensuring that their staff are competent to carry out their responsibilities for safeguarding and promoting the welfare of children and creating an environment where staff feel able to raise concerns and feel supported in their safeguarding role

---

[36] Sir Robert Francis' Freedom to speak up review.

- staff should be given a mandatory induction, which includes familiarisation with child protection responsibilities and the procedures to be followed if anyone has any concerns about a child's safety or welfare

- all practitioners should have regular reviews of their own practice to ensure they have knowledge, skills and expertise that improve over time

People in positions of trust

4.   Organisations and agencies working with children and families should have clear policies for dealing with allegations against people who work with children. Such policies should make a clear distinction between an allegation, a concern about the quality of care or practice or a complaint. An allegation may relate to a person who works with children who has:

- behaved in a way that has harmed a child, or may have harmed a child

- possibly committed a criminal offence against or related to a child

- behaved towards a child or children in a way that indicates they may pose a risk of harm to children

5.   County level and unitary local authorities should ensure that allegations against people who work with children are not dealt with in isolation. Any action necessary to address corresponding welfare concerns in relation to the child or children involved should be taken without delay and in a co-ordinated manner. Local authorities should, in addition, have designated a particular officer, or team of officers (either as part of local multi-agency arrangements or otherwise), to be involved in the management and oversight of allegations against people who work with children. Any such officer, or team of officers, should be sufficiently qualified and experienced to be able to fulfil this role effectively, for example, qualified social workers. Any new appointments to such a role, other than current or former designated officers moving between local authorities, should be qualified social workers. Arrangements should be put in place to ensure that any allegations about those who work with children are passed to the designated officer, or team of officers, without delay.

6.   Local authorities should put in place arrangements to provide advice and guidance to employers and voluntary organisations and agencies on how to deal with allegations against people who work with children. Local authorities should also ensure that there are appropriate arrangements in place to liaise effectively with the police and other organisations and agencies to monitor the progress of cases and ensure that they are dealt with as quickly as possible, consistent with a thorough and fair process.

7.   Employers, school governors, trustees and voluntary organisations should ensure that they have clear policies in place setting out the process, including timescales for investigation and what support and advice will be available to individuals against whom allegations have been made. Any allegation against people who work with children should be reported immediately to a senior manager within the organisation or agency. The designated officer, or team of officers, should also be informed within one working day of all allegations that come to an employer's attention or that are made directly to the police.

8.   If an organisation or agency removes an individual (paid worker or unpaid volunteer) from work in regulated activity[37] with children (or would have, had the person not left first) because the person poses a risk of harm to children, the organisation or agency must make a referral to the Disclosure and Barring Service to consider whether to add the individual to the barred list.

9.   This applies irrespective of whether a referral has been made to local authority children's social care and/or the designated officer or team of officers. It is an offence to fail to make a referral without good reason[38].

Individual organisational responsibilities

10.   In addition to these section 11 duties, which apply to a number of named organisations and agencies, further safeguarding duties are also placed on individual organisations and agencies through other statutes. The key duties that fall on each individual organisation are set out below.

Schools, colleges and other educational providers

11.   The following have duties in relation to safeguarding and promoting the welfare of children:

- governing bodies of maintained schools (including maintained nursery schools), further education colleges and sixth-form colleges[39]

---

[37]Regulated activity in relation to children: scope
[38] Further guidance on referrals to the DBS is available at Appendix B
[39] Further education colleges and sixth-form colleges as established under the Further Education and Higher Education Act 1992 and institutions designated as being withing the further education sector. It relates to their responsibilities towards children who are receiving education or training at the college.

- proprietors of academy schools, free schools, alternative provision academies and non-maintained special schools[40],[41]. In the case of academies and free school trusts, the proprietor will be the trust itself

- proprietors of independent schools

- management committees of pupil referral units[42]

12. This guidance applies in its entirety to all schools.

13. Schools, colleges and other educational settings must also have regard to statutory guidance Keeping Children Safe in Education, which provides further guidance as to how they should fulfil their duties in respect of safeguarding and promoting the welfare of children in their care[43].

Early Years and Childcare

14. Early years providers have a duty under section 40 of the Childcare Act 2006 to comply with the welfare requirements of the early years foundation stage (EYFS)[44]. Early years providers must ensure that:

- they are alert to any issues of concern in the child's life

- they have and implement a policy and procedures to safeguard children. This must include an explanation of the action to be taken when there are safeguarding concerns about a child and in the event of an allegation being made against a member of staff. The policy must also cover the use of mobile phones and cameras in the setting, that staff complete safeguarding training that enables them to understand their safeguarding policy and procedures, have up-to-date knowledge of safeguarding issues, and recognise signs of potential abuse and neglect

- they have a practitioner who is designated to take lead responsibility for safeguarding children within each early years setting and who must liaise with local statutory children's services as appropriate. This lead must also complete child protection training

---

[40] Under the Education (Independent School Standards) (England) Regulations 2014
[41] Under the Education (Non-Maintained Special Schools) (England) Regulations 2011
[42] Section 175, Education Act 2002 for management committees of pupil referral units, this is by virtue of regulation 3 and paragraph 19A of Schedule 1 to the Education (Pupil Referral Units) (Application of Enactments) (England) Regulations 2007.
[43] Keeping Children Safe in Education.
[44] Section 3 – safeguarding and welfare requirements in the Statutory Framework for the Early Years Foundation Stage.

Health

15. Clinical commissioning groups are one of the three statutory safeguarding partners as set out in chapter 3. NHS organisations and agencies are subject to the section 11 duties set out in this chapter. Health practitioners are in a strong position to identify welfare needs or safeguarding concerns regarding individual children and, where appropriate, provide support. This includes understanding risk factors, communicating and sharing information effectively with children and families, liaising with other organisations and agencies, assessing needs and capacity, responding to those needs and contributing to multi-agency assessments and reviews.

16. A wide range of health practitioners have a critical role to play in safeguarding and promoting the welfare of children including: GPs, primary care practitioners, paediatricians, nurses, health visitors, midwives, school nurses, allied health practitioners, those working in maternity, child and adolescent mental health, youth custody establishments, adult mental health, sexual, alcohol and drug services for both adults and children, unscheduled and emergency care settings, highly specialised services and secondary and tertiary care.

17. All staff working in healthcare settings – including those who predominantly treat adults – should receive training to ensure they attain the competences appropriate to their role and follow the relevant professional guidance[45,46,47].

18. Within the NHS[48]:

- **NHS England** is responsible for ensuring that the health commissioning system as a whole is working effectively to safeguard and promote the welfare of children. It is also accountable for the services it directly commissions, including primary care, and healthcare services in the under-18 secure estate (for police custody settings see below in the policing section). NHS England also leads and defines improvement in safeguarding practice and outcomes and should also ensure that there are effective mechanisms for safeguarding partners and Health and wellbeing boards to raise concerns about the engagement and leadership of the local NHS. Each NHSE region should have a safeguarding lead to ensure regional collaboration and assurance through convening safeguarding forums

---

[45] Safeguarding Children and Young People: roles and competences for health care staff, RCPCH (2014).
[46] Looked-after children: Knowledge, skills and competences of health care staff, RCN and RCPCH, (2015).
[47] For example, Protecting children and young people: the responsibilities of all doctors, GMC (2018) and Safeguarding Children and Young People: The RCGP/NSPCC Safeguarding Children Toolkit for General Practice, RCGP (2014).
[48] Further guidance on accountabilities for safeguarding children in the NHS is available in Safeguarding Vulnerable People in the Reformed NHS: Accountability and Assurance Framework (2015).

- Clinical commissioning groups are one of the statutory safeguarding partners and the major commissioners of local health services. They are responsible for the provision of effective clinical, professional and strategic leadership to child safeguarding, including the quality assurance of safeguarding through their contractual arrangements with all provider organisations and agencies, including from independent providers

Designated health professionals

19.   Clinical commissioning groups should employ, or have in place, a contractual agreement to secure the expertise of designated practitioners; such as dedicated designated doctors and nurses for safeguarding children and dedicated designated doctors and nurses for looked-after children (and designated doctor or paediatrician for unexpected deaths in childhood).

20.   In some areas, there will be more than one clinical commissioning group per local authority, and they may consider 'lead' or 'hosting' arrangements for their designated health professionals, or a clinical network arrangement with the number of Designated Doctors and Nurses for child safeguarding equating to the size of the child population[49]. Designated doctors and nurses, as senior professionals, clinical experts and strategic leaders, are a vital source of safeguarding advice and expertise for all relevant organisations and agencies but particularly the clinical commissioning group, NHS England, and the local authority, and for advice and support to other health practitioners across the health economy. The NHS commissioners and providers should ensure that designated professionals are given sufficient time to be fully engaged, involved and included in the new safeguarding arrangements.

21.   All providers of NHS funded health services including NHS Trusts and NHS Foundation Trusts should identify a dedicated named doctor and a named nurse (and a named midwife if the organisation or agency provides maternity services) for safeguarding children. In the case of ambulance trusts and independent providers, this should be a named practitioner. Named practitioners have a key role in promoting good professional practice within their organisation and agency, providing advice and expertise for fellow practitioners, and ensuring safeguarding training is in place. They should work closely with their organisation's/agency's safeguarding lead on the executive board, designated health professionals for the health economy and other statutory safeguarding partners[50].

---

[49] Safeguarding children and young people: roles and competencies for health care staff
[50] Model job descriptions for designated and named professional roles can be found in the intercollegiate document Safeguarding children and young people: roles and competences for health care staff and Safeguarding Children and Young People: The RCGP/NSPCC Safeguarding Children Toolkit for General Practice, RCGP (2014)

22.   Clinical commissioning groups should employ a named GP to advise and support GP safeguarding practice leads. GPs should have a lead and deputy lead for safeguarding, who should work closely with the named GP based in the clinical commissioning group[51].

23.   Other public, voluntary and independent sector organisations, agencies and social enterprises providing NHS services to children and families should ensure that they follow this guidance.

Public Health England

24.   Public Health England (PHE) is an executive agency of the Department of Health and Social Care which has operational autonomy to advise and support government, local authorities and the NHS in a professionally independent manner. PHE's mission is "to protect and improve the nation's health and to address inequalities", and was established in 2013 following the Health and Social Care Act 2012. PHE's Chief Nurse provides advice and expertise in their capacity as the government's professional advisor (Public Health Nursing), which in the context of children's health includes health visitors and school nurses.

Police

25.   The police are one of the three statutory safeguarding partners as set out in chapter 3 and are subject to the section 11 duties set out in this chapter. Under section 1(8)(h) of the Police Reform and Social Responsibility Act 2011, the Police and Crime Commissioner (PCC) must hold the Chief Constable to account for the exercise of the latter's duties in relation to safeguarding children under sections 10 and 11 of the Children Act 2004.

26.   All police officers, and other police employees such as Police Community Support Officers, are well placed to identify early when a child's welfare is at risk and when a child may need protection from harm. Children have the right to the full protection offered by criminal law. In addition to identifying when a child may be a victim of a crime, police officers should be aware of the effect of other incidents which might pose safeguarding risks to children and where officers should pay particular attention. For example, an officer attending a domestic abuse incident should be aware of the effect of such behaviour on any children in the household. Children who are encountered as offenders, or alleged offenders, are entitled to the same safeguards and protection as any other child and due regard should be given to their safety and welfare at all times. For example, children who

---

[51] Intercollegiate framework: Safeguarding children and young people: roles and competencies for healthcare staff

are apprehended in possession of Class A drugs may be victims of exploitation through county lines drug dealing.

27. The police will hold important information about children who may be suffering, or likely to suffer, significant harm, as well as those who cause such harm. They should always share this information with other organisations and agencies where this is necessary to protect children. Similarly, they can expect other organisations and agencies to share information to enable the police to carry out their duties. All police forces should have officers trained in child abuse investigation.

28. The police have a power to remove a child to suitable accommodation under section 46 of the Children Act 1989, if they have reasonable cause to believe that the child would otherwise be likely to suffer significant harm. Statutory powers to enter premises can be used with this section 46 power, and in circumstances to ensure the child's immediate protection. Police powers can help in emergency situations, but should be used only when necessary and, wherever possible, the decision to remove a child from a parent or carer should be made by a court.

29. Restrictions and safeguards exist in relation to the circumstances and periods for which children may be taken to or held in police stations[52]. PCCs are responsible for health commissioning in police custody settings and should always ensure that this meets the needs of individual children.

Adult social care services

30. Local authorities provide services to adults who are themselves responsible for children who may be in need. These services are subject to the section 11 duties set out in this chapter. When staff are providing services to adults they should ask whether there are children in the family and consider whether the children need help or protection from harm. Children may be at greater risk of harm or be in need of additional help in families where the adults have mental health problems, misuse drugs or alcohol, are in a violent relationship, have complex needs or have learning difficulties.

---

[52] Potential powers of entry include those under:
- Police and Criminal Evidence Act 1984 (PACE) section 17(1)(b), a constable may enter and search any premises for the purpose of arresting a person for an indictable offence
- PACE section 17(1)(e), a constable may also enter and search premises for the purpose of saving life or limb or preventing serious damage to property – in the exercise of police protection powers if entry to premises is refused, this section may give adequate powers;
- common law, where a constable has the power to enter premises to prevent or deal with a breach of the peace (which is preserved under PACE section 17(6));
- Children Act 1989 section 48, a warrant may be obtained to search for children who may be in need of emergency protection.

31.   Adults with parental responsibilities for disabled children have a right to a separate parent carer's needs assessment under section 17ZD of the Children Act 1989. Adults who do not have parental responsibility, but are caring for a disabled child, are entitled to an assessment on their ability to provide, or to continue to provide, care for that disabled child under the Carers (Recognition and Services) Act 1995. That assessment must also consider whether the carer works or wishes to work, or whether they wish to engage in any education, training or recreation activities.

32.   Adult social care services should liaise with children's social care services to ensure that there is a joined-up approach when carrying out such assessments.

Housing services

33.   Housing and homelessness services in local authorities and others such as environmental health organisations are subject to the section 11 duties set out in this chapter. Practitioners working in these services may become aware of conditions that could have or are having an adverse impact on children. Under Part 1 of the Housing Act 2004, authorities must take account of the impact of health and safety hazards in housing on vulnerable occupants, including children, when deciding on the action to be taken by landlords to improve conditions. Housing authorities also have an important role to play in safeguarding vulnerable young people, including young people who are pregnant, leaving care or a secure establishment.

British Transport Police

34.   The British Transport Police (BTP) is subject to the section 11 duties set out in this chapter. In its role as the national police for the railways, the BTP can play an important role in safeguarding and promoting the welfare of children, especially in identifying and supporting children who have run away, are truanting from school or who are being exploited by criminal gangs to move drugs and money.

35.   The BTP should carry out its duties in accordance with its legislative powers. This includes removing a child to a suitable place using their police protection powers under the Children Act 1989, and the protection of children who are truanting from school using powers under the Crime and Disorder Act 1998. This involves, for example, the appointment of a designated independent officer in the instance of a child taken into police protection.

Prison Service

36. The Prison Service is subject to the section 11 duties set out in this chapter. It also has a responsibility to identify prisoners who are potential or confirmed 'persons posing a risk to children' (PPRC) and through assessment establish whether the PPRC presents a continuing risk to children whilst in prison custody[53,54]. Where an individual has been identified as a PPRC, the relevant prison establishment:

- should inform the local authority children's social care services of the offender's reception to prison, subsequent transfers, release on temporary licence and of release date and of the release address of the offender

- should notify the relevant probation service provider of PPRC status. The police should also be notified of the release date and address[55,56]

- may prevent or restrict a prisoner's contact with children. Decisions on the level of contact, if any, should be based on a multi-agency risk assessment. The assessment should draw on relevant risk information held by police, the probation service provider and the prison service. The relevant local authority children's social care should contribute to the multi-agency risk assessment by providing a report on the child's best interests. The best interests of the child will be paramount in the decision-making process[57]

37. A prison is also able to monitor an individual's communication (including letters and telephone calls) to protect children where it is proportionate and necessary to the risk presented.

38. Governors/Directors of women's prisons which have Mother and Baby Units (MBUs) should ensure that:

- there is at all times a member of staff allocated to the MBU, who as a minimum, is trained in first aid, whilst within the prison there is always a member of staff on duty who is trained in paediatric first aid (including child/adult resuscitation) who can be called to the MBU if required

- there is a contingency plan/policy in place for child protection, first aid including paediatric first aid and resuscitation, which should include advice for managing

---

[53] This applies not just to adult prisons but also to all types of establishments within the secure estate for children, with the same process applying to children who pose a risk to other children.

[54] HMP Public Protection Manual

[55] Should the PPRC have been released under probation supervision, the prison no longer has responsibility for them and it falls to the NPS/CRC to address and manage the risk in the community.

[56] The management of an individual who presents a risk of harm to children will often be through a multidisciplinary Interdepartmental Risk Management Team (IRMT).

[57] Ministry of Justice Chapter 2, Section 2 of HM Prison Service Public Protection Manual.

such events, and which provides mothers with detailed guidance as to what to do in an emergency

- each baby has a child care plan setting out how the best interests of the child will be maintained and promoted during the child's residence in the unit

This also applies to MBUs which form part of the secure estate for children.

Probation Service

39.   Probation services are provided by the National Probation Service (NPS) and 21 Community Rehabilitation Companies (CRCs). The NPS and CRCs are subject to the section 11 duties set out in this chapter[58]. They are primarily responsible for working with adult offenders both in the community and in the transition from custody to community to reduce reoffending and improve rehabilitation. During the course of their duties, probation staff come into contact with offenders who:

- have offended against a child

- pose a risk of harm to children even though they have not been convicted of an offence against a child

- are parents and/or carers of children

- have regular contact with a child for whom they do not have caring responsibility

They are, therefore, well placed to identify offenders who pose a risk of harm to children as well as children who may be at heightened risk of involvement in, or exposure to, criminal or anti-social behaviour, and of other poor outcomes due to the behaviour and/or home circumstances of their parent/carer(s).

40.   They should ask an offender at the earliest opportunity whether they live with, have caring responsibilities for, are in regular contact with, or are seeking contact with children. Where this applies, a check should be made with the local authority children's services at the earliest opportunity on whether the child/children is/are known to them and, if they are, the nature of their involvement.

41.   Where an adult offender is assessed as presenting a risk of serious harm to children, the offender manager should develop a risk management plan and supervision plan that contains a specific objective to manage and reduce the risk of harm to children. The risk management plan should be shared with other organisations and agencies involved in the risk management.

---

[58] The section 11 duty is conferred on the Community Rehabilitation Companies by virtue of contractual arrangements entered into with the Secretary of State.

42.   In preparing a sentence plan, offender managers should consider how planned interventions might bear on parental responsibilities and whether the planned interventions could contribute to improved outcomes for children known to be in an existing relationship with the offender.

Children's homes

43.   The registered person of a children's home must have regard to the Guide to the Children's Homes Regulations, including the quality standards (April 2015), in interpreting and meeting the Regulations. The Guide covers the quality standards for children's homes, which set out the aspirational and positive outcomes that we expect homes to achieve, including the standard for the protection of children. The registered person is responsible for ensuring that staff continually and actively assess the risks to each child and the arrangements in place to protect them. Where there are safeguarding concerns for a child, their placement plan, agreed between the home and their placing authority, must include details of the steps the home will take to manage any assessed risks on a day to day basis.

44.   In addition to the requirements of this standard, the registered person has specific responsibilities under regulation 34 to prepare and implement policies setting out: arrangements for the safeguarding of children from abuse or neglect; clear procedures for referring child protection concerns to the placing authority or local authority where the home is situated if appropriate; and specific procedures to prevent children going missing and take action if they do.

45.   Each home should work with their local safeguarding partners to agree how they will work together, and with the placing authority, to make sure that the needs of the individual children are met.

The secure estate for children

46.   Governors, managers, directors and principals of the following secure establishments are subject to the section 11 duties set out in this chapter:

- a secure training centre
- a young offender institution
- a secure college/school

47.   Each centre holding those aged under 18 should have in place an annually-reviewed safeguarding children policy. The policy is designed to promote and safeguard the welfare of children and should cover all relevant operational areas as well as key supporting processes, which would include issues such as child protection, risk of harm,

restraint, separation, staff recruitment and information sharing. A manager should be appointed and will be responsible for implementation of this policy[59].

48.   Each centre should work with their local safeguarding partners to agree how they will work together, and with the relevant YOT and placing authority (the Youth Custody Service), to make sure that the needs of individual children are met.

Youth Offending Teams

49.   YOTs are subject to the section 11 duties set out in this chapter. YOTs are multi-agency teams responsible for the supervision of children subject to pre-court interventions and statutory court disposals[60]. They are therefore well placed to identify children known to relevant organisations and agencies as being most at risk of offending and the contexts in which they may be vulnerable to abuse, and to undertake work to prevent them offending or protect them from harm. YOTs should have a lead officer responsible for ensuring safeguarding is embedded in their practice.

50.   Under section 38 of the Crime and Disorder Act 1998, local authorities must, within the delivery of youth justice services, ensure the 'provision of persons to act as appropriate adults to safeguard the interests of children detained or questioned by police officers'.

UK Visas and Immigration, Immigration Enforcement and the Border Force

51.   Section 55 of the Borders, Citizenship and Immigration Act 2009 places upon the Secretary of State a duty to make arrangements to take account of the need to safeguard and promote the welfare of children in discharging functions relating to immigration, asylum, nationality and customs. These functions are discharged on behalf of the Secretary of State by UK Visas and Immigration, Immigration Enforcement and the Border Force, which are part of the Home Office. The statutory guidance Arrangements to Safeguard and Promote Children's Welfare and other guidance relevant to the discharge of specific immigration functions set out these arrangements[61].

---

[59] Detailed guidance on the safeguarding children policy, the roles of the safeguarding children manager and the safeguarding children committee, and the role of the establishment in relation to the LSCB can be found in Prison Service Instruction (PSI) 08/2012 'Care and Management of Young People'.
[60] The statutory membership of YOTs is set out in section 39 (5) of the Crime and Disorder Act 1998.
[61] Arrangements to Safeguard and Promote Children's Welfare in the United Kingdom Border Agency. (original title "Every Child Matters" statutory guidance to the UK Border Agency under section 55 of the Borders, Citizenship and Immigration Act 2009).

Children and Family Court Advisory and Support Service

52.   The responsibility of the Children and Family Court Advisory and Support Service (Cafcass), as set out in the Children Act 1989, is to safeguard and promote the welfare of individual children who are the subject of family court proceedings. This is through the provision of independent social work advice to the court.

53.   A Cafcass officer has a statutory right in public law cases to access local authority records relating to the child concerned and any application under the Children Act 1989. That power also extends to other records that relate to the child and the wider functions of the local authority, or records held by an authorised organisation that relate to that child.

54.   Where a Cafcass officer has been appointed by the court as a child's guardian and the matter before the court relates to specified proceedings, they should be invited to all formal planning meetings convened by the local authority in respect of the child. This includes statutory reviews of children who are accommodated or looked-after, child protection conferences and relevant adoption panel meetings.

Armed Services

55.   Local authorities have the statutory responsibility for safeguarding and promoting the welfare of the children of service families in the UK[62,63]. In discharging these responsibilities:

- local authorities should ensure that the Ministry of Defence, soldiers, sailors, airmen, and Families Association Forces Help, the British Forces Social Work Service or the Naval Personal and Family Service is made aware of any service child who is the subject of a child protection plan and whose family is about to move overseas

- each local authority with a United States (US) base in its area should establish liaison arrangements with the base commander and relevant staff. The requirements of English child welfare legislation should be explained clearly to the US authorities, so that the local authority can fulfil its statutory duties

---

[62] When service families or civilians working with the armed forces are based overseas the responsibility for safeguarding and promoting the welfare of their children is vested in the Ministry of Defence. The Ministry of Defence contact is through the Directorate of Children and Young People: Tel 01980 618710 or email DCYP-DCYP-MAILBOX@mod.uk

[63] The Army welfare contact is through the Army Welfare Service Intake and Assessment Team: Tel. 01904 882053 or email: RC-AWS-IAT-0Mailbox@mod.uk ; The Naval Service welfare contact is through the RN RM Welfare (RNRMW) Portal. Tel: 02392 728777 or email NAVYNPS-PEOPLESTRNRMPORTAL@mod.uk; The RAF welfare contact is through the Personal Support and Social Work Service RAF (SSAFA): Tel: 03000 111 723 or email psswsRAF@ssafa.org.uk

Multi-Agency Public Protection Arrangements

56.   Many of the agencies subject to the section 11 duty are members of the Multi-Agency Public Protection Arrangements (MAPPA), including the police, prison and probation services. MAPPA should work together with duty to co-operate (DTC)[64] agencies to manage the risks posed by violent and sexual offenders living in the community in order to protect the public and should work closely with the safeguarding partners over services to commission locally.

Voluntary, charity, social enterprise, faith-based organisations and private sectors

57.   Voluntary, charity, social enterprise (VCSE) and private sector organisations and agencies play an important role in safeguarding children through the services they deliver. Some of these will work with particular communities, with different races and faith communities and delivering in health, adult social care, housing, prisons and probation services. They may as part of their work provide a wide range of activities for children and have an important role in safeguarding children and supporting families and communities.

58.   Like other organisations and agencies who work with children, they should have appropriate arrangements in place to safeguard and protect children from harm. Many of these organisations and agencies as well as many schools, children's centres, early years and childcare organisations, will be subject to charity law and regulated either by the Charity Commission or other "principal" regulators. Charity trustees are responsible for ensuring that those benefiting from, or working with, their charity, are not harmed in any way through contact with it. The Charity Commission for England and Wales provides guidance on charity compliance which should be followed. Further information on the Charity Commission's role in safeguarding can be found on: the Charity Commission's page on Gov.uk.

59.   Some of these organisations and agencies are large national charities whilst others will have a much smaller local reach. Some will be delivering statutory services and may be run by volunteers, such as library services. This important group of organisations includes youth services not delivered by local authorities or district councils.

60.   All practitioners working in these organisations and agencies who are working with children and their families are subject to the same safeguarding responsibilities, whether paid or a volunteer.

---

[64] The DTC agencies are listed in section 325(6) of the CJA 2003. They are required to co-operate as far as they can do so, consistent with the exercise of their other statutory functions.

61.   Every VCSE, faith-based organisation and private sector organisation or agency should have policies in place to safeguard and protect children from harm. These should be followed and systems should be in place to ensure compliance in this. Individual practitioners, whether paid or volunteer, should be aware of their responsibilities for safeguarding and protecting children from harm, how they should respond to child protection concerns and how to make a referral to local authority children's social care or the police if necessary.

62.   Every VCSE, faith-based organisation and private sector organisation or agency should have in place the arrangements described in this chapter. They should be aware of how they need to work with the safeguarding partners in a local area. Charities (within the meaning of section 1 Charities Act 2011), religious organisations (regulation 34 and schedule 3 to School Admissions) and any person involved in the provision, supervision or oversight of sport or leisure are included within the relevant agency regulations. This means if the safeguarding partners name them as a relevant partner they must cooperate. Other VCSE, faith-based and private sector organisations not on the list of relevant agencies can also be asked to cooperate as part of the local arrangements and should do so.

Sports Clubs / Organisations

63.   There are many sports clubs and organisations including voluntary and private sector providers that deliver a wide range of sporting activities to children. Some of these will be community amateur sports clubs, some will be charities. All should have the arrangements described in this chapter in place and should collaborate to work effectively with the safeguarding partners as required by any local safeguarding arrangements. Paid and volunteer staff need to be aware of their responsibilities for safeguarding and promoting the welfare of children, how they should respond to child protection concerns and how to make a referral to local authority children's social care or the police if necessary.

64.   All National Governing Bodies of Sport, that receive funding from either Sport England[65] or UK Sport[66], must aim to meet the Standards for Safeguarding and Protecting Children in Sport[67].

---

[65] Sport England
[66] UK Sport
[67] Standards for Safeguarding and Protecting Children in Sport.

Chapter 3: Multi-agency safeguarding arrangements

1.	Local organisations and agencies that work with children and families play a significant role when it comes to safeguarding children.

2.	To achieve the best possible outcomes, children and families should receive targeted services that meet their needs in a co-ordinated way. Fragmented provision of services creates inefficiencies and risks disengagement by children and their families from services such as GPs, education and wider voluntary and community specialist support.

3.	There is a shared responsibility between organisations and agencies to safeguard and promote the welfare of all children in a local area.

4.	As set out in chapter 2, many local organisations and agencies have a duty under section 11 of the Children Act 2004 to ensure that they consider the need to safeguard and promote the welfare of children when carrying out their functions.

5.	The responsibility for this join-up locally rests with the three safeguarding partners who have a shared and equal duty to make arrangements to work together to safeguard and promote the welfare of all children in a local area.

Safeguarding partners

Safeguarding partners [68]

A *safeguarding partner* in relation to a local authority area in England is defined under the Children Act 2004 (as amended by the Children and Social Work Act, 2017) as:

(a) the local authority

(b) a clinical commissioning group for an area any part of which falls within the local authority area

(c) the chief officer of police for an area any part of which falls within the local authority area

6.	The three safeguarding partners should agree on ways to co-ordinate their safeguarding services; act as a strategic leadership group in supporting and engaging others; and implement local and national learning including from serious child safeguarding incidents (see chapter 4).

---

[68] Children Act 2004, Section 16E

7.   To fulfil this role, the three safeguarding partners must set out how they will work together and with any relevant agencies. Relevant agencies are those organisations and agencies whose involvement the safeguarding partners consider may be required to safeguard and promote the welfare of children with regard to local need.

8.   The purpose of these local arrangements is to support and enable local organisations and agencies to work together in a system where:

- children are safeguarded and their welfare promoted

- partner organisations and agencies collaborate, share and co-own the vision for how to achieve improved outcomes for vulnerable children

- organisations and agencies challenge appropriately and hold one another to account effectively

- there is early identification and analysis of new safeguarding issues and emerging threats

- learning is promoted and embedded in a way that local services for children and families can become more reflective and implement changes to practice

- information is shared effectively to facilitate more accurate and timely decision making for children and families

9.   In order to work together effectively, the safeguarding partners with other local organisations and agencies should develop processes that:

- facilitate and drive action beyond usual institutional and agency constraints and boundaries

- ensure the effective protection of children is founded on practitioners developing lasting and trusting relationships with children and their families

10.   To be effective, these arrangements should link to other strategic partnership work happening locally to support children and families. This will include other public boards including Health and wellbeing boards, Adult Safeguarding Boards, Channel Panels, Improvement Boards, Community Safety Partnerships, the Local Family Justice Board and MAPPAs.

Leadership

11.   Strong leadership is critical for the new arrangements to be effective in bringing together the various organisations and agencies. It is important therefore that the lead representative from each of the three safeguarding partners plays an active role. The lead representatives for safeguarding partners are: the local authority chief executive, the accountable officer of a clinical commissioning group, and a chief officer of police.

12.   All three safeguarding partners have equal and joint responsibility for local safeguarding arrangements. In situations that require a clear, single point of leadership, all three safeguarding partners should decide who would take the lead on issues that arise.

13.   Should the lead representatives delegate their functions they remain accountable for any actions or decisions taken on behalf of their agency. If delegated, it is the responsibility of the lead representative to identify and nominate a senior officer in their agency to have responsibility and authority for ensuring full participation with these arrangements.

14.   The representatives, or those they delegate authority to, should be able to:

- speak with authority for the safeguarding partner they represent

- take decisions on behalf of their organisation or agency and commit them on policy, resourcing and practice matters

- hold their own organisation or agency to account on how effectively they participate and implement the local arrangements

Geographical area

15.   The geographical footprint for the new arrangements is based on local authority areas. A single local authority area cannot be covered by two separate safeguarding partnerships. Every local authority, clinical commissioning group and police force must be covered by a local safeguarding arrangement. Local arrangements can cover two or more local authorities. Where more than one local authority joins together, the local authorities can agree to delegate their safeguarding partner duties to a single authority[69]. Each local authority must continue to fulfil its statutory and legislative duties to safeguard and promote the welfare of children. The same applies for clinical commissioning groups and chief officers of police (in respect of their safeguarding partner duties only).

16.   The administrative geography of safeguarding partners can be changed over time. Where changes are proposed, these should be agreed by the three safeguarding partners, communicated clearly to relevant agencies and practitioners, and reflected in the next yearly report (see paragraph 42).

---

[69] Children Act 2004, Section 16J

Relevant agencies

17.   As set out below, relevant agencies are those organisations and agencies whose involvement the safeguarding partners consider is required to safeguard and promote the welfare of local children. Strong, effective multi-agency arrangements are ones that are responsive to local circumstances and engage the right people. For local arrangements to be effective, they should engage organisations and agencies that can work in a collaborative way to provide targeted support to children and families as appropriate. This approach requires flexibility to enable joint identification of, and response to, existing and emerging needs, and to agree priorities to improve outcomes for children.

18.   The safeguarding partners must set out in their published arrangements which organisations and agencies they will be working with to safeguard and promote the welfare of children, and this will be expected to change over time if the local arrangements are to work effectively for children and families. A list of relevant agencies is set out in regulations[70].

19.   When selected by the safeguarding partners to be part of the local safeguarding arrangements, relevant agencies must act in accordance with the arrangements[71]. Safeguarding partners should make sure the relevant agencies are aware of the expectations placed on them by the new arrangements. They should consult relevant agencies in developing the safeguarding arrangements to make sure the expectations take account of an agency's structure and statutory obligations.

20.   Where a relevant agency has a national remit, such as the British Transport Police and Cafcass, safeguarding partners should be clear on how these agencies should collaborate and take account of that agency's individual responsibilities and potential contributions towards a number of local safeguarding arrangements. The involvement of health providers and commissioners will be different in each local area and local safeguarding partners should consider how they will secure the clinical expertise of designated health professionals for safeguarding children within their arrangements.

21.   The published arrangements should set out clearly any contributions agreed with relevant agencies, including funding, accommodation, services and any resources connected with the arrangements.

22.   In setting out how they will work with relevant agencies, the safeguarding partners should be clear how they will assure themselves that relevant agencies have appropriate,

---

[70] The Child Safeguarding Practice Review and Relevant Agency (England) Regulations 2018
[71] Children Act 2004, Section 16G

robust safeguarding policies and procedures in place and how information will be shared amongst all relevant agencies and the safeguarding partners.

23.   Many agencies and organisations play a crucial role in safeguarding children. Safeguarding partners may include any local or national organisation or agency in their arrangements, regardless of whether they are named in relevant agency regulations. Organisations and agencies who are not named in the relevant agency regulations, whilst not under a statutory duty, should nevertheless cooperate and collaborate with the safeguarding partners particularly as they may have duties under section 10 and/or section 11 of the Children Act 2004.

24.   Safeguarding partners should communicate regularly with their relevant agencies and others they expect to work with them. It is for the safeguarding partners to determine how regularly their list of relevant agencies will be reviewed. The local arrangements should be shared with all partners and relevant agencies, and information should be given about how to escalate concerns and how any disputes will be resolved. This should give details of the independent scrutiny and whistleblowing procedures.

Schools, colleges and other educational providers

25.   Schools, colleges and other educational providers have a pivotal role to play in safeguarding children and promoting their welfare. Their co-operation and buy-in to the new arrangements will be vital for success. All schools, colleges and other educational providers have duties in relation to safeguarding children and promoting their welfare. The statutory guidance 'Keeping Children Safe in Education' should be read alongside this guidance.

26.   The safeguarding partners should make arrangements to allow all schools (including multi academy trusts), colleges and other educational providers, in the local area to be fully engaged, involved and included in the new safeguarding arrangements. It is expected that local safeguarding partners will name schools, colleges and other educational providers as relevant agencies and will reach their own conclusions on how best locally to achieve the active engagement of individual institutions in a meaningful way.

27.   Once designated as a relevant agency, schools and colleges, and other educational providers, in the same way as other relevant agencies, are under a statutory duty to co-operate with the published arrangements.

Information requests

28.   Organisations and agencies within a strong multi-agency system should have confidence that information is shared effectively, amongst and between them, to improve outcomes for children and their families. Safeguarding partners may require any person or organisation or agency to provide them, any relevant agency for the area, a reviewer or another person or organisation or agency, with specified information. This must be information which enables and assists the safeguarding partners to perform their functions to safeguard and promote the welfare of children in their area, including as related to local and national child safeguarding practice reviews.

29.   The person or organisation to whom a request is made must comply with such a request and if they do not do so, the safeguarding partners may take legal action against them.

30.   As public authorities, safeguarding partners should be aware of their own responsibilities under the relevant information law and have regard to guidance provided by the Information Commissioner's Office when issuing and responding to requests for information.

Independent scrutiny

31.   The role of independent scrutiny is to provide assurance in judging the effectiveness of multi-agency arrangements to safeguard and promote the welfare of all children in a local area, including arrangements to identify and review serious child safeguarding cases[72]. This independent scrutiny will be part of a wider system which includes the independent inspectorates' single assessment of the individual safeguarding partners and the Joint Targeted Area Inspections.

32.   Whilst the decision on how best to implement a robust system of independent scrutiny is to be made locally, safeguarding partners should ensure that the scrutiny is objective, acts as a constructive critical friend and promotes reflection to drive continuous improvement.

33.   The independent scrutineer should consider how effectively the arrangements are working for children and families as well as for practitioners, and how well the safeguarding partners are providing strong leadership and agree with the safeguarding partners how this will be reported.

34.   The published arrangements should set out the plans for independent scrutiny; how the arrangements will be reviewed; and how any recommendations will be taken

---

[72] See chapter 4

forward. This might include, for example, the process and timescales for ongoing review of the arrangements.

35.   Safeguarding partners should also agree arrangements for independent scrutiny of the report they must publish at least once a year (see 'Reporting', below).

Funding

36.   Working in partnership means organisations and agencies should collaborate on how they will fund their arrangements. The three safeguarding partners and relevant agencies for the local authority area should make payments towards expenditure incurred in conjunction with local multi-agency arrangements for safeguarding and promoting welfare of children.

37.   The safeguarding partners should agree the level of funding secured from each partner, which should be equitable and proportionate, and any contributions from each relevant agency, to support the local arrangements. The funding should be transparent to children and families in the area, and sufficient to cover all elements of the arrangements, including the cost of local child safeguarding practice reviews.

Publication of arrangements

38.   Once agreed, local safeguarding arrangements must be published and must include:

- arrangements for the safeguarding partners to work together to identify and respond to the needs of children in the area

- arrangements for commissioning and publishing local child safeguarding practice reviews (see chapter 4)

- arrangements for independent scrutiny of the effectiveness of the arrangements

39.   They should also include:

- who the three local safeguarding partners are, especially if the arrangements cover more than one local authority area

- geographical boundaries (especially if the arrangements operate across more than one local authority area)

- the relevant agencies the safeguarding partners will work with; why these organisations and agencies have been chosen; and how they will collaborate and work together to improve outcomes for children and families

- how all early years settings, schools (including independent schools, academies and free schools) and other educational establishments will be included in the safeguarding arrangements

- how any youth custody and residential homes for children will be included in the safeguarding arrangements

- how the safeguarding partners will use data and intelligence to assess the effectiveness of the help being provided to children and families, including early help

- how inter-agency training will be commissioned, delivered and monitored for impact and how they will undertake any multiagency and interagency audits

- how the arrangements will be funded

- the process for undertaking local child safeguarding practice reviews, setting out the arrangements for embedding learning across organisations and agencies,

- how the arrangements will include the voice of children and families

- how the threshold document[73] setting out the local criteria for action aligns with the arrangements

Dispute resolution

40.   Safeguarding partners and relevant agencies must act in accordance with the arrangements for their area, and will be expected to work together to resolve any disputes locally. Public bodies that fail to comply with their obligations under law are held to account through a variety of regulatory and inspection activity. In extremis, any non-compliance will be referred to the Secretary of State.

Reporting

41.   In order to bring transparency for children, families and all practitioners about the activity undertaken, the safeguarding partners must publish a report at least once in every 12-month period. The report must set out what they have done as a result of the arrangements, including on child safeguarding practice reviews, and how effective these arrangements have been in practice.

42.   In addition, the report should also include:

---

[73] see Chapter 1: Assessing need and providing help

- evidence of the impact of the work of the safeguarding partners and relevant agencies, including training, on outcomes for children and families from early help to looked-after children and care leavers

- an analysis of any areas where there has been little or no evidence of progress on agreed priorities

- a record of decisions and actions taken by the partners in the report's period (or planned to be taken) to implement the recommendations of any local and national child safeguarding practice reviews, including any resulting improvements

- ways in which the partners have sought and utilised feedback from children and families to inform their work and influence service provision

43.   Safeguarding partners should make sure the report is widely available, and the published safeguarding arrangements should set out where the reports will be published.

44.   A copy of all published reports should be sent to the Child Safeguarding Practice Review Panel[74] and the What Works Centre for Children's Social Care within seven days of being published.

45.   Where there is a secure establishment in a local area, safeguarding partners should include a review of the use of restraint within that establishment in their report, and the findings of the review should be reported to the Youth Justice Board.

46.   The three safeguarding partners should report any updates to the published arrangements in their yearly report and the proposed timescale for implementation.

---

[74] Children Act 2004, Section 16F (3)(c)

Chapter 4: Improving child protection and safeguarding practice

Overview

1.   Child protection in England is a complex multi-agency system with many different organisations and individuals playing their part. Reflecting on how well that system is working is critical as we constantly seek to improve our collective public service response to children and their families.

2.   Sometimes a child suffers a serious injury or death as a result of child abuse or neglect. Understanding not only what happened but also why things happened as they did can help to improve our response in the future. Understanding the impact that the actions of different organisations and agencies had on the child's life, and on the lives of his or her family, and whether or not different approaches or actions may have resulted in a different outcome, is essential to improve our collective knowledge. It is in this way that we can make good judgments about what might need to change at a local or national level.

Purpose of child safeguarding practice reviews

3.   The purpose of reviews of serious child safeguarding cases, at both local and national level, is to identify improvements to be made to safeguard and promote the welfare of children. Learning is relevant locally, but it has a wider importance for all practitioners working with children and families and for the government and policy-makers. Understanding whether there are systemic issues, and whether and how policy and practice need to change, is critical to the system being dynamic and self-improving.

4.   Reviews should seek to prevent or reduce the risk of recurrence of similar incidents. They are not conducted to hold individuals, organisations or agencies to account, as there are other processes for that purpose, including through employment law and disciplinary procedures, professional regulation and, in exceptional cases, criminal proceedings. These processes may be carried out alongside reviews or at a later stage. Employers should consider whether any disciplinary action should be taken against practitioners whose conduct and/or practice falls below acceptable standards and should refer to their regulatory body as appropriate.

Responsibilities for reviews

5.   The responsibility for how the system learns the lessons from serious child safeguarding incidents lies at a national level with the Child Safeguarding Practice Review Panel (the Panel) and at local level with the safeguarding partners.

6.   The Panel is responsible for identifying and overseeing the review of serious child safeguarding cases which, in its view, raise issues that are complex or of national importance. The Panel should also maintain oversight of the system of national and local reviews and how effectively it is operating.

7.   Locally, safeguarding partners must make arrangements to identify and review serious child safeguarding cases which, in their view, raise issues of importance in relation to their area. They must commission and oversee the review of those cases, where they consider it appropriate for a review to be undertaken.

8.   The Panel and the safeguarding partners have a shared aim in identifying improvements to practice and protecting children from harm and should maintain an open dialogue on an ongoing basis. This will enable them to share concerns, highlight commonly-recurring areas that may need further investigation (whether leading to a local or national review), and share learning, including from success, that could lead to improvements elsewhere.

9.   Safeguarding partners should have regard to any guidance which the Panel publishes. Guidance will include the timescales for rapid reviews (see paragraph 20) and for the Panel response.

10.   Serious child safeguarding cases are those in which:

- abuse or neglect of a child is known or suspected **and**

- the child has died or been seriously harmed

11.   Serious harm includes (but is not limited to) serious **and/or** long-term impairment of a child's mental health or intellectual, emotional, social or behavioural development. It should also cover impairment of physical health[75]. This is not an exhaustive list. When making decisions, judgment should be exercised in cases where impairment is likely to be long-term, even if this is not immediately certain. Even if a child recovers, including from a one-off incident, serious harm may still have occurred.

---

[75] Child perpetrators may also be the subject of a review, if the definition of 'serious child safeguarding case' is met.

Duty on local authorities to notify incidents to the Child Safeguarding Practice Review Panel

> **16C(1) of the Children Act 2004 (as amended by the Children and Social Work Act 2017) states:**
>
> Where a local authority in England knows or suspects that a child has been abused or neglected, the local authority must notify the Child Safeguarding Practice Review Panel if –
>
> (a) the child dies or is seriously harmed in the local authority's area, or
>
> (b) while normally resident in the local authority's area, the child dies or is seriously harmed outside England.

12. The local authority must notify any event that meets the above criteria to the Panel[76]. They should do so within five working days of becoming aware that the incident has occurred. The local authority should also report the event to the safeguarding partners in their area (and in other areas if appropriate[77]) within five working days.

13. The local authority must **also** notify the Secretary of State and Ofsted where a looked after child has died, whether or not abuse or neglect is known or suspected.

14. The duty to notify events to the Panel rests with the local authority. Others who have functions relating to children[78] should inform the safeguarding partners of any incident which they think should be considered for a child safeguarding practice review. Contact details and notification forms for local authorities to notify incidents to the Panel are available from the notification to Ofsted page on Gov.uk[79].

Decisions on local and national reviews

15. Safeguarding partners must make arrangements to:

- identify serious child safeguarding cases which raise issues of importance in relation to the area **and**

---

[76] Online notifications to the Panel will be shared with Ofsted (to inform its inspection and regulatory activity) and with DfE to enable it to carry out its functions.

[77] If, for example, the event relates to a looked after child who has been placed out of area.

[78] This means any person or organisation with statutory or official duties or responsibilities relating to children.

[79] This form will be replaced later in 2018 with a new notification system.

- commission and oversee the review of those cases, where they consider it appropriate for a review to be undertaken

16.   When a serious incident becomes known to the safeguarding partners[80], they must consider whether the case meets the criteria for a local review.

17.   Meeting the criteria does not mean that safeguarding partners must automatically carry out a local child safeguarding practice review. It is for them to determine whether a review is appropriate, taking into account that the overall purpose of a review is to identify improvements to practice. Issues might appear to be the same in some child safeguarding cases but reasons for actions and behaviours may be different and so there may be different learning to be gained from similar cases. Decisions on whether to undertake reviews should be made transparently and the rationale communicated appropriately, including to families.

18.   Safeguarding partners must consider the criteria and guidance below when determining whether to carry out a local child safeguarding practice review.

The criteria which the local safeguarding partners must take into account include whether the case[81]:
• highlights or may highlight improvements needed to safeguard and promote the welfare of children, including where those improvements have been previously identified
• highlights or may highlight recurrent themes in the safeguarding and promotion of the welfare of children
• highlights or may highlight concerns regarding two or more organisations or agencies working together effectively to safeguard and promote the welfare of children
• is one which the Child Safeguarding Practice Review Panel have considered and concluded a local review may be more appropriate

---

[80] Safeguarding partners should also take account of information from other sources if applicable.
[81] The Child Safeguarding Practice Review and Relevant Agency (England) Regulations 2018.

Safeguarding partners should also have regard to the following circumstances:

- where the safeguarding partners have cause for concern about the actions of a single agency

- where there has been no agency involvement and this gives the safeguarding partners cause for concern

- where more than one local authority, police area or clinical commissioning group is involved, including in cases where families have moved around

- where the case may raise issues relating to safeguarding or promoting the welfare of children in institutional settings[82]

19.   Some cases may not meet the definition of a 'serious child safeguarding case', but nevertheless raise issues of importance to the local area. That might, for example, include where there has been good practice, poor practice or where there have been 'near miss' events. Safeguarding partners may choose to undertake a local child safeguarding practice review in these or other circumstances.

The rapid review

20.   The safeguarding partners should promptly undertake a rapid review of the case, in line with any guidance published by the Panel. The aim of this rapid review is to enable safeguarding partners to:

- gather the facts about the case, as far as they can be readily established at the time

- discuss whether there is any immediate action needed to ensure children's safety and share any learning appropriately

- consider the potential for identifying improvements to safeguard and promote the welfare of children

- decide what steps they should take next, including whether or not to undertake a child safeguarding practice review

21.   As soon as the rapid review is complete, the safeguarding partners should send a copy to the Panel[83]. They should also share with the Panel their decision about whether a

---

[82] Includes children's homes (including secure children's homes) and other settings with residential provision for children; custodial settings where a child is held, including police custody, young offender institutions and secure training centres; and all settings where detention of a child takes place, including under the Mental Health Act 1983 or the Mental Capacity Act 2005.

[83] The Panel may share this with DfE if requested, to enable DfE to carry out its functions.

local child safeguarding practice review is appropriate, or whether they think the case may raise issues which are complex or of national importance such that a national review may be appropriate. They may also do this if, during the course of a local child safeguarding practice review, new information comes to light which suggests that a national review may be appropriate. As soon as they have determined that a local review will be carried out, they should inform the Panel, Ofsted and DfE, including the name of any reviewer they have commissioned.

Guidance for the national Child Safeguarding Practice Review Panel

22. On receipt of the information from the rapid review, the Panel must decide whether it is appropriate to commission a national review of a case or cases. They must consider the criteria and guidance below.

The criteria which the Panel must take into account include whether the case[84]:

- highlights or may highlight improvements needed to safeguard and promote the welfare of children, including where those improvements have been previously identified

- raises or may raise issues requiring legislative change or changes to guidance issued under or further to any enactment

- highlights or may highlight recurrent themes in the safeguarding and promotion of the welfare of children

The Panel should also have regard to the following circumstances:

- significant harm or death to a child educated otherwise than at school

- where a child is seriously harmed or dies while in the care of a local authority, or while on (or recently removed from) a child protection plan

- cases which involve a range of types of abuse[85]

- where the case may raise issues relating to safeguarding or promoting the welfare of children in institutional settings[86]

---

[84] The Child Safeguarding Practice Review and Relevant Agency (England) Regulations 2018

[85] For example, trafficking for the purposes of child sexual exploitation.

[86] Includes children's homes (including secure children's homes) and other settings with residential provision for children; custodial settings where a child is held, including police custody, young offender institutions and secure training centres; and all settings where detention of a child takes place, including under the Mental Health Act 1983 or the Mental Capacity Act 2005.

23.   As well as considering notifications from local authorities and information from rapid reviews and local child safeguarding practice reviews, the Panel should take into account a range of other evidence, including inspection reports and other reports and research. The Panel may also take into account any other criteria they consider appropriate to identify whether a serious child safeguarding case raises issues which are complex or of national importance.

24.   In many cases there will need to be dialogue between the safeguarding partners and the Panel to support the decision-making process. The safeguarding partners must share further information with the Panel as requested.

25.   The Panel should inform the relevant safeguarding partners promptly following receipt of the rapid review, if they consider that:

- a national review is appropriate, setting out the rationale for their decision and next steps

- further information is required to support the Panel's decision-making (including whether the safeguarding partners have taken a decision as to whether to commission a local review)

26.   The Panel should take decisions on whether to undertake national reviews and communicate their rationale appropriately, including to families. The Panel should notify the Secretary of State when a decision is made to carry out a national review.

27.   If the Panel decides to undertake a national review they should discuss with the safeguarding partners the potential scope and methodology of the review and how they will engage with them and those involved in the case.

28.   There will be instances where a local review has been carried out which could then form part of a thematic review that the Panel undertakes at a later date. There may also be instances when a local review has not been carried out but where the Panel considers that the case could be helpful to a national review at some stage in the future. In such circumstances, the Panel should engage with safeguarding partners to agree the conduct of the review.

29.   Alongside any national or local reviews, there could be a criminal investigation, a coroner's investigation and/or professional body disciplinary procedures. The Panel and the safeguarding partners should have clear processes for how they will work with other investigations, including Domestic Homicide Reviews, multi-agency public protection arrangements reviews or Safeguarding Adults Reviews, and work collaboratively with those responsible for carrying out those reviews. This is to reduce burdens on and anxiety for the children and families concerned and to minimise duplication of effort and uncertainty.

Commissioning a reviewer or reviewers for a local child safeguarding practice review

30.   The safeguarding partners are responsible for commissioning and supervising reviewers for local reviews[87].

31.   In all cases they should consider whether the reviewer has the following:

- professional knowledge, understanding and practice relevant to local child safeguarding practice reviews, including the ability to engage both with practitioners and children and families

- knowledge and understanding of research relevant to children's safeguarding issues

- ability to recognise the complex circumstances in which practitioners work together to safeguard children

- ability to understand practice from the viewpoint of the individuals, organisations or agencies involved at the time rather than using hindsight

- ability to communicate findings effectively

- whether the reviewer has any real or perceived conflict of interest

Local child safeguarding practice reviews

32.   The safeguarding partners should agree with the reviewer(s) the method by which the review should be conducted, taking into account this guidance and the principles of the systems methodology recommended by the Munro review[88]. The methodology should provide a way of looking at and analysing frontline practice as well as organisational structures and learning. The methodology should be able to reach recommendations that will improve outcomes for children. All reviews should reflect the child's perspective and the family context.

33.   The review should be proportionate to the circumstances of the case, focus on potential learning, and establish and explain the reasons why the events occurred as they did.

34.   As part of their duty to ensure that the review is of satisfactory quality, the safeguarding partners should seek to ensure that:

---

[87] Safeguarding partners may also consider appointing reviewers from the Child Safeguarding Practice Review Panel's pool of reviewers where available.
[88] The Munro Review of Child Protection: Final Report: A Child Centred System (May 2011).

- practitioners are fully involved in reviews and invited to contribute their perspectives without fear of being blamed for actions they took in good faith

- families, including surviving children, are invited to contribute to reviews. This is important for ensuring that the child is at the centre of the process[89]. They should understand how they are going to be involved and their expectations should be managed appropriately and sensitively

35.   The safeguarding partners must supervise the review to ensure that the reviewer is making satisfactory progress and that the review is of satisfactory quality. The safeguarding partners may request information from the reviewer during the review to enable them to assess progress and quality; any such requests must be made in writing. The President of the Family Division's guidance covering the role of the judiciary in SCRs[90] should also be noted in the context of child safeguarding practice reviews.

Expectations for the final report

36.   Safeguarding partners must ensure that the final report includes:

- a summary of any recommended improvements to be made by persons in the area to safeguard and promote the welfare of children

- an analysis of any systemic or underlying reasons why actions were taken or not in respect of matters covered by the report

37.   Any recommendations should be clear on what is required of relevant agencies and others collectively and individually, and by when, and focussed on improving outcomes for children.

38.   Reviews are about promoting and sharing information about improvements, both within the area and potentially beyond, so safeguarding partners must publish the report, unless they consider it inappropriate to do so. In such a circumstance, they must publish any information about the improvements that should be made following the review that they consider it appropriate to publish. The name of the reviewer(s) should be included. Published reports or information must be publicly available for at least one year.

39.   When compiling and preparing to publish the report, the safeguarding partners should consider carefully how best to manage the impact of the publication on children, family members, practitioners and others closely affected by the case. The safeguarding

---

[89] Morris, K., Brandon, M., and Tudor, P., (2013) 'Rights, Responsibilities and Pragmatic Practice: Family participation in Case Reviews'.
[90] President of the Family Division's Guidance covering the role of the judiciary in serious case reviews.

partners should ensure that reports are written in such a way so that what is published avoids harming the welfare of any children or vulnerable adults involved in the case.

40.   Safeguarding partners must send a copy of the full report to the Panel and to the Secretary of State no later than seven working days[91] before the date of publication. Where the safeguarding partners decide only to publish information relating to the improvements to be made following the review, they must also provide a copy of that information to the Panel and the Secretary of State within the same timescale. They should also provide the report, or information about improvements, to Ofsted within the same timescale.

41.   Depending on the nature and complexity of the case, the report should be completed and published as soon as possible and no later than six months from the date of the decision to initiate a review. Where other proceedings may have an impact on or delay publication, for example an ongoing criminal investigation, inquest or future prosecution, the safeguarding partners should inform the Panel and the Secretary of State of the reasons for the delay. Safeguarding partners should also set out for the Panel and the Secretary of State the justification for any decision not to publish either the full report or information relating to improvements. Safeguarding partners should have regard to any comments that the Panel or the Secretary of State may make in respect of publication.

42.   Every effort should also be made, both before the review and while it is in progress, to (i) capture points from the case about improvements needed, and (ii) take corrective action and disseminate learning.

Actions in response to local and national reviews

43.   The safeguarding partners should take account of the findings from their own local reviews and from all national reviews, with a view to considering how identified improvements should be implemented locally, including the way in which organisations and agencies work together to safeguard and promote the welfare of children. The safeguarding partners should highlight findings from reviews with relevant parties locally and should regularly audit progress on the implementation of recommended improvements[92]. Improvement should be sustained through regular monitoring and follow up of actions so that the findings from these reviews make a real impact on improving outcomes for children.

---

[91] 'Working day' means any day which is not a Saturday, Sunday or Bank Holiday.
[92] See also paragraph 41 in chapter 3 (safeguarding partners' report).

Guidance for the Child Safeguarding Practice Review Panel – reviewers

44.   The Panel must set up a pool of potential reviewers who can undertake national reviews, a list of whom must be publicly available. If they consider that there are no potential reviewers in the pool with availability or suitable experience to undertake the review, they may select a person who is not in the pool. When selecting a reviewer, the Panel should consider whether they have any conflict of interest which could restrict their ability, or perceived ability, to identify improvements impartially.

45.   For national child safeguarding practice reviews, the Panel should follow the same guidance on procedure and supervision as for local child safeguarding practice reviews (paragraphs 32-35).

The Panel – expectations for the final report

46.   The Panel must ensure that the final report includes:

- a summary of any improvements being recommended to the safeguarding partners and/or others to safeguard and promote the welfare of children

- an analysis of any systemic or underlying reasons why actions were taken or not taken in respect of matters covered by the report

47.   The Panel must publish the report, unless they consider it inappropriate to do so. In such a circumstance they must publish any information about the improvements that should be made following the review that they consider it appropriate to publish. The name of the reviewer(s) should be included.

48.   The Panel should work with safeguarding partners to identify and manage the impact of the publication on children, family members, practitioners and others closely affected by the case.

49.   The Panel must ensure that reports or information published are publicly available for at least three years. The Panel must send a copy of the full report to the Secretary of State no later than seven working days before the date of publication. Where the Panel decides only to publish information relating to the improvements to be made following the review, they must also provide a copy of that information to the Secretary of State within the same timescale. The Panel should also send a copy of the report or improvements to the relevant safeguarding partners, Ofsted, the Care Quality Commission and Her Majesty's Inspectorate of Constabulary and Fire & Rescue Services.

50.   Reports should be completed and published within six months of the date of the decision to initiate a review. Where other proceedings may have an impact on or delay

publication, for example an ongoing criminal investigation, inquest or future prosecution, the Panel should advise the Secretary of State of the reasons for the delay. The Panel should also set out for the Secretary of State the explanation for any decision not to publish either the full report or information relating to improvements. During the review, the Panel should share any points that arise about improvements needed with the safeguarding partners in any local authority areas covered by the review and others as applicable.

51.   The Panel should send copies of published reports of national and local child safeguarding practice reviews, or published information relating to improvements that should be made following those reviews, to the What Works Centre for Children's Social Care and relevant inspectorates, bodies or individuals as they see fit. Where a local review results in findings which are of national importance, or in recommendations for national government, the Panel should consider the potential of those recommendations to improve systems to safeguard and promote the welfare of children and how best to disseminate and embed such learning.

Chapter 5: Child death reviews

1.   The death of a child is a devastating loss that profoundly affects all those involved. The process of systematically reviewing the deaths of children is grounded in respect for the rights of children and their families[93], with the intention of learning what happened and why, and preventing future child deaths.

2.   The majority of child deaths in England arise from medical causes. Enquiries should keep an appropriate balance between forensic and medical requirements and supporting the family at a difficult time. This chapter provides guidance to child death review partners in light of their statutory responsibilities.

3.   Child death review partners are local authorities and any clinical commissioning groups for the local area as set out in the Children Act 2004 (the Act), as amended by the Children and Social Work Act 2017[94]. The statutory responsibilities for child death review partners are set out in the table below, and the boundaries for child death review partners should be decided locally as described in paragraph 9 of this chapter.

4.   In the immediate aftermath of a child's death, a copy of *When a Child Dies – a guide for families and carers*[95] should be offered to all bereaved families or carers in order to support them through the child death review process. In addition to supporting families and carers, staff involved in the care of the child should also be considered and offered appropriate support.

---

[93] United Nations Convention on the Rights of the Child
[94] Sections 16Q
[95] *When a Child Dies – a guide for families and carers*

Statutory Requirements[96]

When a child dies, in any circumstances, it is important for parents and families to understand what has happened and whether there are any lessons to be learned.

The responsibility for ensuring child death reviews are carried out is held by 'child death review partners,' who, in relation to a local authority area in England, are defined as the local authority for that area and any clinical commissioning groups operating in the local authority area.

Child death review partners must make arrangements to review all deaths of children normally resident in the local area[97] and, if they consider it appropriate, for any non-resident child who has died in their area.

Child death review partners for two or more local authority areas may combine and agree that their areas be treated as a single area for the purpose of undertaking child death reviews.

Child death review partners must make arrangements for the analysis of information from all deaths reviewed.

The purpose of a review and/or analysis is to identify any matters relating to the death, or deaths, that are relevant to the welfare of children in the area or to public health and safety, and to consider whether action should be taken in relation to any matters identified. If child death review partners find action should be taken by a person or organisation, they must inform them. In addition, child death review partners:

- must, at such times as they consider appropriate, prepare and publish reports on:

  - what they have done as a result of the child death review arrangements in their area, and

  - how effective the arrangements have been in practice;

- may request information from a person or organisation for the purposes of enabling or assisting the review and/or analysis process - the person or organisation must comply with the request, and if they do not, the child death review partners may take legal action to seek enforcement: and

- may make payments directly towards expenditure incurred in connection with arrangements made for child death reviews or analysis of information about deaths reviewed, or by contributing to a fund out of which payments may be made; and may provide staff, goods, services, accommodation or other resources to any person for purposes connected with the child death review or analysis process.

---

[96] The guidance in this chapter is issued under section 16Q of the Children Act 2004. Further guidance on child death review procedures will be issued by the government. While the contents of this chapter will be duplicated within that document, child death review partners should also have regard to that guidance to assist in their understanding of the steps taken by others prior to the child death reviews and analysis they carry out.

[97] For the purposes of child death reviews, a local area is the area within the remit of a local authority (referred to in the Act as a "local authority area").

Responsibilities of Child Death Review Partners

5.   The child death review process covers children: a child is defined in the Act as a person under 18 years of age[98], regardless of the cause of death[99].

6.   In making arrangements to review child deaths, child death review partners should establish a structure and process to review all deaths of children normally resident in their area and, if appropriate and agreed between child death review partners, the deaths of children not normally resident in their area but who have died there. Child death review partners may, if they consider it appropriate, model their child death review structures and processes on the current Child Death Overview Panel (CDOP) framework[100].

7.   The child death review partners should consider the core representation of any panel or structure they set up to conduct reviews and this would ideally include: public health; the designated[101] doctor for child deaths for the local area; social services; police; the designated doctor or nurse for safeguarding; primary care (GP or health visitor); nursing and/or midwifery; lay representation; and other professionals that child death review partners consider should be involved. It is for child death review partners to determine what representation they have in any structure reviewing child deaths.

8.   Child death review partners should agree locally how the child death review process will be funded in their area.

9.   The geographical and population 'footprint' of child death review partners should be locally agreed, but must extend to at least one local authority area. This footprint should take into account networks of NHS care, and agency and organisational boundaries in order to reflect the integrated care and social networks of the local area. These may overlap with more than one local authority area or clinical commissioning group. They should cover a child population such that they typically review at least 60 child deaths per year. Child death review partners should come together to develop clear plans outlining the administrative and logistical processes for these new review arrangements.

10.   Child death review partners should ensure that a designated doctor for child deaths is appointed to any multi-agency panel (or structure in place to review deaths). The designated doctor for child deaths should be a senior paediatrician who can take a lead role in the review process. Child death review partners should ensure a process is in

---

[98] Section 65 of the Children Act 2004.

[99] This will include the death of any new-born baby (of any gestation) who shows signs of life following birth, or where the birth was unattended, but does not include those (of any gestation) who are stillborn or where there was medical attendance, or planned terminations of pregnancy carried out within the law.

[100] The CDOP frameworks were established and are currently used by Local Safeguarding Children Boards to review the deaths of children in their areas.

[101] Within that part of the health system that supports child safeguarding and protection services, the word "designated" means a dedicated professional with specific roles and responsibilities that are centred on the provision of clinical expertise and strategic advice.

place whereby the designated doctor for child deaths is notified of each child death and is sent relevant information.

11. Child death review partners may request a person or organisation to provide information to enable or assist the reviewing and/or analysing of a child's death. The person or organisation to whom a request is made must comply with such a request and if they do not do so, the child death review partners may instigate legal action to enforce.

12. Child death review partners for the local authority area where a child who has died was normally resident are responsible for ensuring the death is reviewed. However, they may also choose to review the death of a child in their local area even if that child is not normally resident there. Child death review partners may wish to consider this for the deaths of looked-after children in their area who were not normally resident there. The review process should seek to involve child death review partners for another local authority area who had an interest in the child or any other person or agencies, as appropriate.

13. Child death review partners should publicise information on the arrangements for child death reviews in their area. This should include who the accountable officials are (the local authority chief executive and the accountable officer of the clinical commissioning group), which local authority and clinical commissioning group partners are involved, what geographical area is covered and who the designated doctor for child deaths is.

Responsibilities of other organisations and agencies

14. All local organisations or individual practitioners that have had involvement in the case should co-operate, as appropriate, in the child death review process carried out by child death review partners. All local organisations or individual practitioners should also have regard to any guidance on child death reviews issued by the government.

Specific responsibilities of relevant bodies in relation to child deaths	
Registrars of Births and Deaths (Section 31 of the Children and Young Persons Act 2008)	Requirement on registrars of births and deaths to supply child death review partners with the particulars of the death entered in the register in relation to any person who was or may have been under the age of 18 at the time of death. A similar requirement exists where the registrar corrects an entry in the register.

| | The registrar must also notify child death review partners if they issue a Certificate of No Liability to Register (where a death is not required by law to be registered in England or Wales) where it appears that the deceased was or may have been under the age of 18 at the time of death.

The information must be provided to the appropriate child death review partners (which cover the sub-district in which the register is kept) no later than seven days from either the date the death was registered, the date the correction was made or the date the certificate was issued[102]. |
|---|---|
| Coroners and Justice Act 2009

Coroners (Investigations) Regulations 2013 | Duty to investigate and hold an inquest. Powers to request a post-mortem and for evidence to be given or produced.

Coroner's duty to notify the child death review partners[103] for the area in which the child died or where the child's body was found within three working days of deciding to investigate a death or commission a post-mortem.

Coroner's duty to share information with the relevant child death review partners[104]. |

---

[102]Amendments have been made to the Children and Young Persons Act. It should be noted that while these amendments came into force on 29th June 2018, they will not have effect in a local authority area until the date that area implements its new safeguarding partnership arrangements.

[103] Amendments will be made to the Coroners (Investigations) Regulations 2013 to require the Coroner to notify the relevant safeguarding partners and child death review partners instead of LSCBs. Until such time as these amendments are made, where a local area has implemented its new safeguarding partnership arrangements, Coroners are asked to also notify relevant child death review partners.

[104] Amendments will be made to the (Investigations) Regulations 2013 to require the Coroner to share information with the relevant safeguarding partners and child death review partners instead of LSCBs. Until such time as these amendments are made, where a local area has implemented its new safeguarding partnership arrangements, Coroners are asked to also share information with the relevant child death review partners.

Responding to the death of a child: the child death review process

Flow Chart 7: Process to follow when a child dies

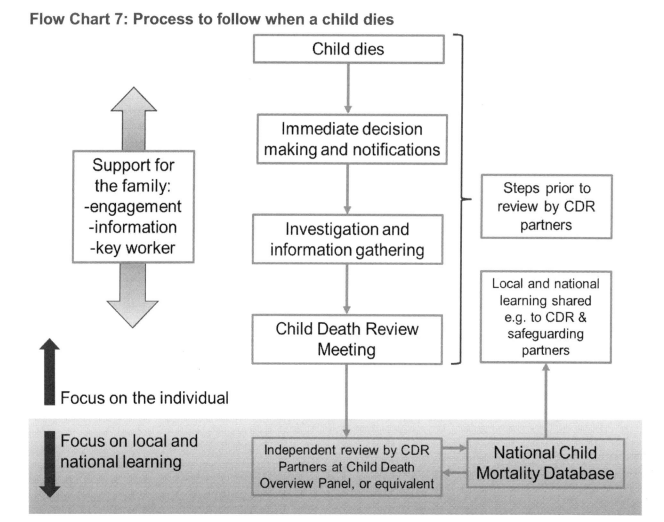

Figure 1. Chart illustrating the full process of a child death review. This includes both the statutory responsibilities of Child Death Review partners to review the deaths of children (described here as review at CDOP or equivalent), and the processes that precede or follow this independent review. Further explanation is below.

15.   The *steps that precede* the child death review partners' independent review (figure 1), commence in the immediate aftermath of a child's death. These include the immediate decisions, notifications and parallel investigations, and the local case review by those directly involved with the care of the child or involved in the investigation after death, at the Child Death Review Meeting. The information gathered throughout this process should be fed into the partners' review.

16.   The learning from all child death reviews should be shared with the National Child Mortality Database, once operational, which may in addition take into account information from other reviews in order to identify any trends or similarities with deaths. Information

from the database may be able to inform systematic or local changes to prevent future deaths. See paragraph 27 for transitional arrangements for the database.

17.   The processes that should be followed by all those involved when responding to, investigating, and reviewing all child deaths is set out in the further guidance on child death reviews issued by the government.

18.   All practitioners participating in the child death review process should notify, report, and scrutinise child deaths using the standardised templates. These should be forwarded to the relevant CDOP (or other structure child death review partners have put in place to help review child deaths). The mechanism for collecting this data will evolve as the National Child Mortality Database becomes operational.

The child death review process

A child dies

19.   Practitioners in all agencies should notify the local child death review partners, via the local CDOP administrator (or equivalent) of the death of any child of which they become aware by using the notification form.

Immediate decision making and notifications & Investigation and information gathering

20.   Whenever a child dies, practitioners should work together in responding to that death in a thorough, sensitive and supportive manner. The aims of this response are to:

- establish, as far as is possible, the cause of the child's death
- identify any modifiable contributory factors[105]
- provide ongoing support to the family
- learn lessons in order to reduce the risk of future child deaths and promote the health, safety and wellbeing of other children
- ensure that all statutory obligations are met

21.   Where a Joint Agency Response is required, practitioners should follow the process set out in *Sudden and Unexpected Death in Infancy and Childhood: multiagency guidelines for care and investigation (2016)*. A Joint Agency Response is required if a child's death:

- is or could be due to external causes
- is sudden and there is no immediately apparent cause (including sudden

---

[105] These are defined as factors which may have contributed to the death of the child and which might, by means of a locally or nationally achievable intervention, be modified to reduce the risk of future deaths.

unexpected death in infancy/childhood)

- ☐ occurs in custody, or where the child was detained under the Mental Health Act

- ☐ occurs where the initial circumstances raise any suspicions that the death may not have been natural

- ☐ occurs in the case of a stillbirth where no healthcare professional was in attendance

22.   If there is an unexplained death of a child at home or in the community, the child should normally be taken to an emergency department rather than a mortuary. In some cases when a child dies at home or in the community, the police may decide that it is not appropriate to move the child's body immediately, for example, because forensic examinations are needed.

23.   In a criminal investigation, the police are responsible for collecting and collating all relevant information pertaining to the child's death. Practitioners should consult the lead police investigator and the Crown Prosecution Service to ensure that their enquiries do not prejudice any criminal proceedings.

24.   If the results of any investigations suggest evidence of abuse or neglect as a possible cause of death, the paediatrician should inform relevant safeguarding partners and the Child Safeguarding Practice Review Panel immediately.

Child Death Review Meeting

25.   This is the multi-professional meeting that takes place prior to the child death review partners review. At the meeting, all matters relating to an individual child's death are discussed by professionals involved with the case. The child death review meeting should be attended by professionals who were directly involved in the care of that child during his or her life and in the investigation into his or her death, and should not be limited to medical staff. A draft analysis form of each individual case should be sent from the child death review meeting to child death review partners to inform the independent review at a CDOP, or equivalent.

Review of death by child death review partners

26.   The review by the child death review partners (at CDOP, or equivalent), is intended to be the final, independent scrutiny of a child's death by professionals with no responsibility for the child during their life. The information gathered using all the standardised templates may help child death review partners to identify modifiable factors that could be altered to prevent future deaths.

27.   In addition to the statutory purposes set out above, the review should also provide

data[106] to NHS Digital and then, once established, to the National Child Mortality Database.

28.   Child death review partners for a local authority area in England must prepare and publish a report as set out in the statutory responsibilities above. They may therefore wish to ask the CDOP (or equivalent) to produce an annual report for child death review partners on local patterns and trends in child deaths, any lessons learnt and actions taken, and the effectiveness of the wider child death review process in order to assist child death review partners to prepare their report.

---

[106] Specified data to NHS Digital for the transitional period will be notified to Child Death Review partners separately. The mechanism for collecting, and the content of, this data will evolve as the National Child Mortality Database becomes operational.

Appendix A: Glossary

Item	Definition
Children	Anyone who has not yet reached their 18th birthday. The fact that a child has reached 16 years of age, is living independently or is in further education, is a member of the armed forces, is in hospital or in custody in the secure estate, does not change their status or entitlements to services or protection.
Safeguarding and promoting the welfare of children	Defined for the purposes of this guidance as: a. protecting children from maltreatment b. preventing impairment of children's health or development c. ensuring that children are growing up in circumstances consistent with the provision of safe and effective care d. taking action to enable all children to have the best outcomes
Child protection	Part of safeguarding and promoting welfare. This refers to the activity that is undertaken to protect specific children who are suffering, or are likely to suffer, significant harm.
Abuse	A form of maltreatment of a child. Somebody may abuse or neglect a child by inflicting harm, or by failing to act to prevent harm. Children may be abused in a family or in an institutional or community setting by those known to them or, more rarely, by others. Abuse can take place wholly online, or technology may be used to facilitate offline abuse. Children may be abused by an adult or adults, or another child or children.
Physical abuse	A form of abuse which may involve hitting, shaking, throwing, poisoning, burning or scalding, drowning, suffocating or otherwise causing physical harm to a child. Physical harm may also be caused when a parent or carer fabricates the symptoms of, or deliberately induces, illness in a child.

Item	Definition
Emotional abuse	The persistent emotional maltreatment of a child such as to cause severe and persistent adverse effects on the child's emotional development. It may involve conveying to a child that they are worthless or unloved, inadequate, or valued only insofar as they meets the needs of another person. It may include not giving the child opportunities to express their views, deliberately silencing them or 'making fun' of what they say or how they communicate. It may feature age or developmentally inappropriate expectations being imposed on children. These may include interactions that are beyond a child's developmental capability, as well as overprotection and limitation of exploration and learning, or preventing the child participating in normal social interaction. It may involve seeing or hearing the ill-treatment of another. It may involve serious bullying (including cyber bullying), causing children frequently to feel frightened or in danger, or the exploitation or corruption of children. Some level of emotional abuse is involved in all types of maltreatment of a child, though it may occur alone.
Sexual abuse	Involves forcing or enticing a child or young person to take part in sexual activities, not necessarily involving a high level of violence, whether or not the child is aware of what is happening. The activities may involve physical contact, including assault by penetration (for example, rape or oral sex) or non-penetrative acts such as masturbation, kissing, rubbing and touching outside of clothing. They may also include non-contact activities, such as involving children in looking at, or in the production of, sexual images, watching sexual activities, encouraging children to behave in sexually inappropriate ways, or grooming a child in preparation for abuse Sexual abuse can take place online, and technology can be used to facilitate offline abuse. Sexual abuse is not solely perpetrated by adult males. Women can also commit acts of sexual abuse, as can other children.
Child sexual exploitation	Child sexual exploitation is a form of child sexual abuse. It occurs where an individual or group takes advantage of an imbalance of power to coerce, manipulate or deceive a child or young person under the age of 18 into sexual activity (a) in exchange for something the victim needs or wants, and/or (b) for the financial advantage or increased status of the perpetrator or facilitator. The victim may have been sexually exploited even if the sexual activity appears consensual. Child sexual exploitation does not always involve physical contact; it can also occur through the use of technology.

Item	Definition
Neglect	The persistent failure to meet a child's basic physical and/or psychological needs, likely to result in the serious impairment of the child's health or development. Neglect may occur during pregnancy as a result of maternal substance abuse. Once a child is born, neglect may involve a parent or carer failing to: a. provide adequate food, clothing and shelter (including exclusion from home or abandonment) b. protect a child from physical and emotional harm or danger c. ensure adequate supervision (including the use of inadequate care-givers) d. ensure access to appropriate medical care or treatment It may also include neglect of, or unresponsiveness to, a child's basic emotional needs.
Extremism	Extremism goes beyond terrorism and includes people who target the vulnerable – including the young – by seeking to sow division between communities on the basis of race, faith or denomination; justify discrimination towards women and girls; persuade others that minorities are inferior; or argue against the primacy of democracy and the rule of law in our society. Extremism is defined in the Counter Extremism Strategy 2015 as the vocal or active opposition to our fundamental values, including the rule of law, individual liberty and the mutual respect and tolerance of different faiths and beliefs. We also regard calls for the death of members of our armed forces as extremist.
Young carer	A young carer is a person under 18 who provides or intends to provide care for another person (of any age, except generally where that care is provided for payment, pursuant to a contract or as voluntary work).
Parent carer	A person aged 18 or over who provides or intends to provide care for a disabled child for whom the person has parental responsibility.
Education, Health and Care Plan	A single plan, which covers the education, health and social care needs of a child or young person with special educational needs and/or a disability (SEND). See the Special Educational Needs and Disability Code of Practice 0-25 (2014).

Item	Definition
Local authority designated officer	County level and unitary local authorities should ensure that allegations against people who work with children are not dealt with in isolation. Any action necessary to address corresponding welfare concerns in relation to the child or children involved should be taken without delay and in a coordinated manner. Local authorities should, in addition, have designated a particular officer, or team of officers (either as part of multi-agency arrangements or otherwise), to be involved in the management and oversight of allegations against people who work with children. Any such officer, or team of officers, should be sufficiently qualified and experienced to be able to fulfil this role effectively, for example qualified social workers. Any new appointments to such a role, other than current or former designated officers moving between local authorities, should be qualified social workers. Arrangements should be put in place to ensure that any allegations about those who work with children are passed to the designated officer, or team of officers, without delay.
Safeguarding partners	A *safeguarding partner* in relation to a local authority area in England is defined under the Children Act 2004 as: (a) the local authority, (b) a clinical commissioning group for an area any part of which falls within the local authority area, and (c) the chief officer of police for an area any part of which falls within the local authority area. The three safeguarding partners should agree on ways to co-ordinate their safeguarding services; act as a strategic leadership group in supporting and engaging others; and implement local and national learning including from serious child safeguarding incidents. To fulfil this role, the three safeguarding partners must set out how they will work together and with any relevant agencies as well as arrangements for conducting local reviews.
Child death review partners	A child death review partner in relation to a local authority area in England is defined under the Children Act 2004 as (a) the local authority, and (b) any clinical commissioning group for an area any part of which falls within the local authority area. The two partners must make arrangements for the review of each death of a child normally resident in the area and may also, if they consider it appropriate, make arrangements for the review of a death in their area of a child not normally resident there. They must also make arrangements for the analysis of information about deaths reviewed under this section. The purposes of a review or analysis are (a) to identify any matters relating to the death or deaths that are relevant to the welfare of

Item	Definition
	children in the area or to public health and safety, and (b) to consider whether it would be appropriate for anyone to take action in relation to any matters identified.
County Lines	As set out in the Serious Violence Strategy, published by the Home Office, a term used to describe gangs and organised criminal networks involved in exporting illegal drugs into one or more importing areas within the UK, using dedicated mobile phone lines or other form of 'deal line'. They are likely to exploit children and vulnerable adults to move and store the drugs and money, and they will often use coercion, intimidation, violence (including sexual violence) and weapons.
Child criminal exploitation	As set out in the Serious Violence Strategy, published by the Home Office, where an individual or group takes advantage of an imbalance of power to coerce, control, manipulate or deceive a child or young person under the age of 18 into any criminal activity (a) in exchange for something the victim needs or wants, and/or (b) for the financial or other advantage of the perpetrator or facilitator and/or (c) through violence or the threat of violence. The victim may have been criminally exploited even if the activity appears consensual. Child criminal exploitation does not always involve physical contact; it can also occur through the use of technology.

Appendix B: Further sources of information

Department for Education guidance

- Care of unaccompanied migrant children and child victims of modern slavery
- Child sexual exploitation: definition and guide for practitioners
- Children Act 1989: care planning, placement and case review
- Children Act 1989: court orders
- Children Act 1989: private fostering
- Information sharing: advice for practitioners providing safeguarding services
- Keeping children safe in education: for schools and colleges
- Knowledge and skills statements for child and family social work
- Listening to and involving children and young people Department for Education and Home Office
- Mandatory reporting of female genital mutilation: procedural information Department for Education and Home Office
- Multi-agency statutory guidance on female genital mutilation Department for Education, Department of Health and Social Care, and Home Office
- National action plan to tackle child abuse linked to faith or belief
- National minimum standards for private fostering
- Non-Maintained Special Schools Regulations 2015
- Pathways to harm, pathways to protection: a triennial analysis of serious case reviews, 2011 to 2014
- Preventing and tackling bullying
- Safeguarding children Department for Education, Home Office, Ofsted, Department of Health and Social Care, Ministry of Housing, Communities & Local Government, Care Quality Commission, Department for Digital, Culture, Media & Sport, and Foreign & Commonwealth Office
- Safeguarding Children in whom illness is fabricated or induced Department for Education, Department of Health and Social Care and Home Office
- Safeguarding children who may have been trafficked Department for Education and Home Office
- Safeguarding strategy - unaccompanied asylum seeking and refugee children
- Sexual violence and sexual harassment between children in schools and colleges
- Statutory framework for the early years [under 5s] foundation stage (EYFS)
- Statutory guidance on children who run away or go missing from home or care

- ☐ Statutory visits to children with special educational needs and disabilities or health conditions in long-term residential settings Department for Education and Department of Health and Social Care.

- ☐ The Child Safeguarding Practice Review and Relevant Agency (England) Regulations 2018

- ☐ The prevent duty: for schools and childcare providers

- ☐ United Nations Convention on the rights of the child

- ☐ Use of reasonable force in schools

- ☐ Visiting children in residential special schools and colleges Department for Education and Department of Health and Social Care

- ☐ What to do if you're worried a child is being abused: advice for practitioners

Guidance issued by other government departments and agencies

- ☐ Achieving Best Evidence in Criminal Proceedings: Guidance on interviewing victims and witnesses, and guidance on using special measures Ministry of Justice

- ☐ Advice to parents and carers on gangs Home Office

- ☐ Advice to schools and colleges on gangs and youth violence Home Office

- ☐ Apply for a forced marriage protection order Foreign & Commonwealth Office

- • Arrangements to Safeguard and Promote Children's Welfare (original title "Every Child Matters") UK Visas and Immigration

- ☐ Asset Plus: assessment and planning in the youth justice system Youth Justice Board

- ☐ Carers Strategy: Second National Action Plan 2014-2016 Department of Health and Social Care

- ☐ Carers Strategy: the second national action plan 2014-2016 Department of Health and Social Care

- ☐ Channel Duty guidance - Protecting vulnerable people from being drawn into terrorism Home Office

- ☐ Criminal exploitation of children and vulnerable adults: county lines Home Office

- ☐ Cyber Aware National Cyber Security Centre

- ☐ DBS barring referral guidance Disclosure and Barring Service

- ☐ Developing local substance misuse safeguarding protocols Public Health England

- ☐ Disclosure and Barring Services Disclosure and Barring Service

- ☐ Female Genital Mutilation Protection Orders: factsheet Home Office

- ☐ Forced marriage Foreign & Commonwealth Office and Home Office

- ☐ Forced Marriage Protection Orders HM Courts & Tribunals Service

- ☐ Guidance for health professionals on domestic violence Department of Health and Social Care

- Handling cases of forced marriage: multi-agency practice guidelines Foreign & Commonwealth Office

- Indecent images of children guidance for young people Home Office

- Mental Health Act 1983 Code of Practice: Guidance on the visiting of psychiatric patients by children Department of Health

- Mental Health Act 1983 Code of Practice: Guidance on the visiting of psychiatric patients by children Department of Health

- Missing Children and Adults - A Cross Government Strategy Home Office

- Modern slavery Act statutory guidance Home Office

- Multi-agency public protection arrangements (MAPPA) Ministry of Justice, National Offender Management Service, and HM Prison Service

- National service framework: children, young people and maternity services Department of Health and Social Care

- NHS England safeguarding Policy NHS England

- Prison, probation and rehabilitation: Public protection manual National Offender Management Service and HM Prison Service

- Probation service guidance on conducting serious further offence reviews framework Ministry of Justice

- Radicalisation - Prevent strategy Home Office

- Recognised, valued and supported: next steps for the carers strategy 2010 Department of Health and Social Care

- Safeguarding vulnerable people in the reformed NHS: Accountability and Assurance Framework NHS England

- Serious and Organised Crime Toolkit: An Interactive Toolkit for practitioners working with young people Home Office

- Thinkuknow [Supporting children to stay safe online] National Crime Agency

- Understanding the female genital mutilation enhanced dataset: updated guidance and clarification to support implementation Department of Health and Social Care

- Violence against women and girls Home Office

Guidance issued by external organisations

- Child maltreatment: when to suspect maltreatment in under 18s NICE

- Child protection and the Dental Team British Dental Association

- Children's Commissioner

- Children's rights and the law - Children's Rights Alliance for England

- Cyberbullying: Understand, Prevent, Respond – Guidance for Schools Childnet International

- How we protect children's rights – Unicef

- ☐ Inter parental relationships Early Intervention Foundation
- ☐ NICE guideline on child abuse and neglect NICE
- • Prison and Probation Ombudsman's fatal incidents investigation
- ☐ Private fostering CoramBAAF
- ☐ Protecting children and young people: doctors' responsibilities General Medical Council
- ☐ Safeguarding Children Toolkit for General Practice Royal College of General Practitioners
- ☐ Standards for safeguarding and protecting children in sport NSPCC
- ☐ Sudden unexpected death in infancy and childhood: multi-agency guidelines for care and investigation Royal College of Pathologists
- ☐ Whistleblowing advice line NSPCC
- ☐ Working Together with Parents Network update of the DoH/DfES Good practice guidance on working with parents with a learning disability (2007) University of Bristol

About this publication:

enquiries: www.education.gov.uk/contactus
download www.gov.uk/government/publications

Reference: DFE-00195-2018

 Follow us on Twitter:
@educationgovuk

 Like us on Facebook:
facebook.com/educationgovuk

Printed in Great
Britain
by Amazon